Correctional Issues

Community Corrections

ACA

FOUNDED 1870

American Correctional Association Staff:

Bobbie L. Huskey, President
James A. Gondles, Jr., Executive Director
Gabriella M. Daley, Director, Communications and Publications
Leslie A. Maxam, Assistant Director, Communications and Publications
Alice Fins, Publications Managing Editor
Michael Kelly, Associate Editor
Mike Selby, Production Editor
Tracie D. Garrett, Production Assistant
Cover art by Morgan Graphics, Takoma Park, Maryland
Printed in the United States by Graphics Communications Inc.

This publication may be ordered from:
The American Correctional Association
4380 Forbes Boulevard
Lanham, Maryland 20706-4322
1-800-ACA-JOIN

Library of Congress Cataloging-in-Publication Data:
Correctional issues: community corrections.
    p.   cm.
        Includes bibliographical references (p.).
        ISBN 1-56991-045-6 (pbk.)
    1. Community-based corrections—United States. 2. Alternatives to imprisonment—United States. I. American Correctional Association.
HV9279.C67 1996   96-21018
364.6'8--dc20   CIP

Table of Contents

Electronic Monitoring

Foreword

We are pleased to bring you this issue of Correctional Issues that discusses the array of community corrections options. It is the belief of the American Correctional Association that rather than building new facilities, greater use should be made of community corrections. This option is not only more cost effective, it frees up needed space for violent criminals.

It is testimony to the creativity and innovation of corrections professionals working with the public that the variety of community corrections options is growing. In fact, we have just published a whole book on boot camps: *Juvenile and Adult Boot Camps*, another community corrections option.

Many of the essays in this volume originally appeared in *Corrections Today* or in the *ACA Proceedings: The State of Corrections*. However, most were extensively updated and revised to be able to provide readers with current, useful information that will enable them to keep up to date and design options in their own community based on the models and suggestions in this volume.

There is an extensive section in this volume that concerns electronic monitoring. Originally, we were going to publish a separate monograph on this, but we thought that since it was so closely tied to the whole of community corrections that it belonged in this work. That section provides the history of electronic monitoring, the development of American Correctional Association standards for electronic monitoring, and several examples of the ways that communities are employing electronic monitoring.

James A. Gondles, Jr.
Executive Director
American Correctional Association

Introduction

Community corrections is a difficult term to define. Community corrections' programs deal with persons under the control of the courts who are not placed in correctional institutions. Community concepts such as intermediate sanctions, alternatives to incarceration, probation and parole, offender residential treatment centers and pretrial release all can be placed under the umbrella of community corrections.

Community corrections' programs can address adjudication initiatives such as pretrial release programs where defendants are not yet found guilty, but are placed under community supervision by the courts. However, most commonly, the term is applied to programs that deal with convicted offenders who are supervised in the community as part of their court-imposed sanction. Offenders may be returning to the community after having been in a correctional institution (in other words, on parole) or they may be serving a court-imposed sentence in the community (probation).

No matter what motives are behind the programs, since the days of John Augustus, the seventeenth century father of probation, rehabilitation, and supervision, several themes characterize community corrections' programs: we must address what caused the criminality, supervise the offender in the community to assure treatment compliance and so that there is no repetition of criminal behavior and the public safety is assured.

A vast number of community corrections programs are the responsibility of parole and probation agencies. These agencies act as the arm of the court or paroling authorities. They provide the courts and paroling authorities with information and act in their behalf by carrying out their mandates. There are also a number of community corrections programs that are the responsibility of departments of corrections such as prerelease programs. Additionally, some courts have created pretrial release agencies that are separate from probation agencies and report directly to the courts. Additionally, there are combinations of these. Yet, the structure of authority can be vastly different depending on the jurisdiction.

Specific community corrections' programs also can be implemented in many different ways. Private and nonprofit companies have contracted out with government agencies to implement a wide variety of community corrections' programs. Private and nonprofit vendors provide treatment and residential services as well as supervision services for the offender population in the community. These organizations can provide specific expertise to the offender population that government agencies cannot. They can offer supplemental services to enhance supervision plans and provide an array of services at a better cost and with specific expertise.

Contracting out for specific community services is quite common among agencies responsible for community corrections' program plans.

In today's environment of increased incarceration for violent offenders, community corrections' programs will play a vital role in the total criminal justice spectrum. Incarceration is an expensive method of dealing with the offender population. Even if there is increased use of incarceration, offenders will require some form of postrelease supervision to provide a transition back into the community. Additionally, jurisdictions will become more selective on just exactly whom they want to incarcerate and for how long. Violent offenders are already a target population for increased incarceration and for longer terms. However, nonviolent offenders can and will be effectively supervised in the community.

The future of community corrections' programs will need to address issues of accountability and retribution and the traditional themes of rehabilitation and supervision. A new community corrections' concept such as restorative justice is taking hold in a number of jurisdictions across the country. This concept is routed in the community and uses community corrections' programs for implementation. The idea is to hold offenders accountable and engage them in repairing the community from the damage done by their acts. This allows victims some form of compensation, offender accountability, and direct offender involvement with the community to experience first hand types are being targeted for these programs. Public safety, retribution, and punishment are integral parts of these programs.

The collection of abstracts in this work describes community corrections' issues from the specific to the conceptual. The American Correctional Association (ACA) has adopted a Community Corrections Policy Statement which contains elements of what all good community corrections programs should contain (see page 133). Issues not only dealing with the offender but with the community, public safety, and proper planing are discussed within the policy. This policy statement was developed as a guideline for those persons implementing community corrections' programs. ACA also has developed a Resolution on Community Corrections that calls on policymakers to implement and support community corrections' initiatives (see page 135).

Several well-written abstracts address various conceptual elements of community corrections' programs. Gail Hughes, Deputy Director of the Missouri Department of Corrections is a recognized leader in community corrections. He describes the major players needed for implementing community corrections' programs. He discusses how members of the judiciary, parole boards, institutional administrators, and community corrections' program implementers need to work hand-in-hand to develop effective communication, goals and strategies for successful programs. Donald Evans, of Ontario, Canada also talks about the importance of involving probation departments and the community in a collaborative effort. Public education is the first step in gaining support for community corrections' initiatives, especially with probation agencies, which are the ones charged with implementing community corrections' programs. John Larivee, with the Crime and Justice Foundation in Boston, presents an interesting abstract about the benefits of reintegration programs. He, too, talks about the importance of documenting successes through an emphasis on outcome measures. Community corrections' programs have more responsibility to ensure success of clients than to just assess and refer. Success depends on following through and ultimate outcomes.

Dennis Schrantz of Michigan, in his "The Five Tenets of Effective Community Corrections," discusses critical concepts that should be included in the development of community corrections' programs. In "Optimal Conditions for Community Corrections," Dr. Roger Lauen and Brad Bogue write that community corrections "must be more than a sophisticated social control strategy." They explain that participation of a wide band of community members is necessary to guide offenders along a new path, otherwise such programs will have only a limited impact.

The next category of abstracts discusses organizational goals of community corrections' programming. Brendan Reynolds, of the Correctional Service of Canada (CSC), discusses the Canadian experience with alternatives to incarceration. The Canadian experience is based on ongoing research on the successes or failures of their initiatives. Donald J. Hengesh provides a view into existing community corrections' programs used by the state of Michigan Department of Corrections, including boot camps, intensive supervision, and electronic monitoring. These programs are presented in terms of new prison construction not being the only way out of a problem. M. Patrick McCabe, Director of Correctional Services for the Salvation Army, presents a very interesting abstract on the history of their organization's 131 year involvement in corrections.

Local jurisdictions operating jails have been in the forefront of developing innovative community corrections initiatives. Neil E. Dorsey from the Montgomery County, Maryland Department of Corrections and Rehabilitation presents his county's perspective on community corrections. Their county, a suburb of Washington, D.C., has a large general population. Their programs deal with diversion and pretrial and sentenced offender populations.

Another group of abstracts deals with specific programs in community corrections. Elizabeth L. Curtin from the Crime and Justice Foundation describes the Metropolitan Day Reporting Center in Boston along with a historical and philosophical perspective on day reporting centers. Richard J. Maher, a United States Probation Officer, details a community service program operating in Atlanta, Georgia. He presents specific projects and the dollars saved for each. He provides a brief perspective of federal sentencing guidelines and the context within which community service programs fit into them. Cary W. Harkaway, Deputy Director Multnomah County Department of Community Corrections in Portland, Oregon describes a correctional literacy program operating in the community for probationers. The program was developed as a result of a fundamental recognition that basic education was a main stumbling block for economic stability for a significant number of people on probation. The program is described in sufficient detail for those interested in replication initiatives. Another abstract describes several programs operating in South Carolina that concern strategies to impact on parole violators. Richard P. Stroker of the South Carolina Department of Probation, Parole and Pardon Services describes how parole violations were impacting on prison overcrowding and the initiatives taken by South Carolina to deal with this issue. The resulting strategies were enacted to address violations from front-end decision making to supervision to creating a violation framework by which officers were to operate. They established a set of guidelines that provide more structure to the violation process that can be traced so that everyone knows what the next step is in the process. Early results were encouraging as to the impact these programs have had on the overcrowding problem and the revocation rates.

Annesley K. Schmidt is the foremost expert in the use and development of electronic monitoring equipment in the country. I do not believe there is anyone who is as expert on this subject as she. Her article, "Electronic Monitoring: Past, Present, and Future" is very informative, even for the experienced user of electronic monitoring equipment. It is written to benefit the uninformed reader as well as the seasoned veteran in community corrections. A description of electronic monitoring and its history provide a sound basis for understanding its applicability in corrections. Aspects of electronic monitoring are presented in the form of its current diversity. The article's presentation of the future raises interesting questions about where technology can take correctional supervision in the community. She describes the various types of electronic monitoring equipment at the end of the article. This provides valuable information for the reader as it points out the capabilities and cost implications for the different types of equipment. It is not so much a question of how we can use the equipment, it is how can the equipment support what we want to accomplish.

David Savage describes electronic monitoring in the Washington State Department of Corrections. His article presents a unique approach to technology and the public/private sector relationship. Washington State Department of Corrections, Community Corrections Division has had an electronic monitoring program in existence for quite some time. Their implementation strategy has been interesting. He points out some of the goals and realities of their programs and the difficulties they have experienced.Their unique approach to resolving some of these problems through a public/private partnership can be a lesson for other practitioners.

In his article, Ray Wahl asks is electronic home monitoring a viable option? He points out some very important issues that need to be examined prior to any decision to begin an electronic monitoring program. Each jurisdiction is different. No two criminal justice systems are alike. Whether local, state, or federal, reasons for particular practices are unique to that community. This article points out the importance of examining those issues and incorporating them into the decision–making process when developing these programs. Additionally, Mr. Wahl talks about some of the wrong reasons, in his opinion, for implementing an electronic monitoring program. He also discusses issues of net widening and cost factors. Terrance F. Lang's article is primarily about an evaluation of the intensive supervision electronic monitoring program in Saskatchewan, Canada. The successes of the program are documented and the program goals are presented. The Canadian approach to intensive supervision and electronic monitoring is more than a supervision and control perspective. There is an accepted notion that an examination of the issues that caused the criminal behavior must be addressed in the implementation strategy of intensive supervision and electronic monitoring. The author believes that community corrections cannot only survive in the "get tough" sentiment but has a place and should be presented in the context of a sanction continuum. He presents electronic monitoring and intensive supervision as a viable sanction option for the courts.

Jim Putnam's article describes the state of Michigan's experience with electronic monitoring from its infancy to its anticipated future. The author describes how Michigan initially became involved with one of the first vendors dealing with electronic monitoring equipment in 1986. He describes the initial perception and technology hurdles, and the evolution of its use in Michigan. Through this he demonstrates how perseverance and determination can work in creating a viable and thriving concept. He also describes how electronic monitoring expanded within the state to other uses and populations within the criminal justice system. He presents cost factors as well as data regarding recidivism and violations. As a result of positive experience, the confidence factor has increased significantly with the courts and the community. He also touches upon a new generation of electronic monitoring capabilities. The author anticipates that emerging technology will further expand its use for community supervision while allowing for improved monitoring and supervision.

Former ACA President, Perry Johnson's article talks about the Michigan experience with electronic monitoring and provides a different viewpoint. The author presents a brief history of the Michigan experience, giving the reader the rationale used for the initial impetus. His perspective is from a political leadership point of view. This perspective takes into consideration the political realities facing Michigan at the time. This is an important perspective as it relates to the correctional leadership implications needed prior to implementation of these types of initiatives. He presents the particulars of the Michigan program and five critical elements for a successful program. The author's view is that electronic monitoring in and of itself is not a program, but a tool to be used within the context of a program. He provides cost implications and recommendations for reader consideration when exploring the implementation of an electronic monitoring program.

Bruce Orenstein
Community Corrections Specialist, ACA

Closing the Loop: A Continuum of Care for Community Corrections

Donald J. Hengesh

Clinton County Sheriff
St. Johns, Michigan

We cannot build our way out of prison crowding. Michigan is just completing an $853 million building project, adding 15,000 beds, doubling capacity. When Michigan is finished building, population projections show, it will be 15,000 beds short. Ohio, Illinois, Florida, California, and many other states have had similar experiences after massive building projects. As taxpayers, we cannot afford to pay for more construction, let alone the costs of operating more prisons.

There is a very definite need for prisons. Some people need to be isolated from society for our protection. However, leaders in corrections need to provide the courts and the public with a system of high-quality, credible, cost-effective community-based programs that close the loop between traditional probation and prison. This paper describes three such programs: "boot camps," or special alternative incarceration, intensive supervision, and electronic monitoring, or "tethering," as some call it.

Boot Camps

Boot camps are one of the waves in corrections today. Used as a diversion from prison, they are cost effective and give offenders the opportunity to learn things that prison would not teach them. Offenders typically are incarcerated for 90 to 120 days compared to one or more years in prison. Studies show boot camp recidivism rates to be between 25 and 30 percent. These rates are comparable to those of traditional probation and parole.

The intent of boot camps is to build within the offender self-discipline, individual responsibility, and a solid work ethic. This is done through strict discipline, hard work, physical training, and academic and life skills programming.

Critics of the program ask, "How can you change someone or build self-esteem when you are yelling at them and calling them such derogatory names?" This yelling is part of the intake process that strips away street-tough attitudes that young offenders bring in with them. The boot camp process is something like a building project on a city lot that is covered with trash. You first have to clear away the trash before you can start building. That clearing away of the trash is what happens during intake. Those street attitudes, macho images, language, and hairstyle, are all stripped away. Then, during the course of the next eleven weeks or so, we construct a foundation on which others can build—a foundation of self-esteem, self-discipline, and responsibility.

In looking at boot camps or shock incarceration units, one needs to look not only at the discipline and physical rigors of the program, but at its real intent. These programs are not designed to make the offender a whole person in just ninety days. They are designed to teach those basic skills of self-discipline and self-esteem that, in turn, can get the offender ready to accept community-based treatment programs such as probation supervision, drug counseling, academic and vocational programming, and work, all of which the offender has rejected in the past. A key element in making shock incarceration work is community aftercare. For a fuller discussion of boot camps see the American Correctional Association's 1996 publication: *Juvenile and Adult Boot Camps*.

Intensive Supervision

When offenders leave a shock incarceration program, a halfway house, or a substance abuse treatment center, they have learned how to function with external application of discipline and structure. However, they have not learned how to apply that discipline or structure themselves in a free community. For offenders to make a successful transition and continue building themselves into productive citizens, they need intensive supervision. Intensive supervision is not just a large number of contacts ensuring that offenders are complying with their parole or probation orders. With intensive supervision, parole and probation officers take responsibility for their cases and their outcomes. This requires involvement and intervention.

In the seventies, parole and probation officers became "brokers of service." They went from being everything to the offender—counselor, employment specialist, financial adviser, and more—to referring the offender to outside agencies for all those services. With increasing caseloads, the brokering of services became an efficient way of dealing with the large numbers of offenders. However, with this brokering of services and large caseloads, parole and probation officers lost their personal involvement in the outcome of the case and became more and more dependent on the service providers to do that. In many instances, the parole and probation officers almost have become clerks, making referrals and logging contacts.

For intensive supervision to work, it takes more than brokering services. Caseloads need to be a size, thirty to thirty-five cases, where the officer gets to know the offenders and what their needs are and then has the time to broker the needed services. The officer needs to have regular contacts with each offender, following up to see that the offender is going to work, going to counseling, and staying away from substance abuse. The officer needs to talk with the offender to see if there are any problems developing. If there are, the officer should intervene by helping the offender resolve the problem. All this takes the officer's involvement. It also takes correctional management to provide the needed resources, time, staff training, equipment, and funds to purchase needed services.

Critics of intensive supervision say that because of the close supervision, more violations are found, and subsequently, more offenders are sent to prison. That does not need to be and should not be the case. If the officer is involved in managing the case, violations will be found, but, hopefully, at an early stage when intervention is possible and a more serious violation necessitating prison can be averted.

Critics also say that intensive supervision is expensive. Yes, it is expensive but not as expensive as prison. With an average prison cost of $25,000 a year per offender, the diversion of three offenders from prison would pay the costs of a parole or probation officer and provide dollars for services. One intensive officer in the course of a year in turn, could supervise approximately seventy-five to ninety cases. If those same seventy-five cases were in prison for a year, it would cost $1,875,000. Intensive supervision is cost-effective, but for the public, law enforcement, and the courts to accept it, it has to be tough and credible.

Electronic Monitoring

One way to enhance intensive supervision, and in many instances free up jail space, is by the use of electronic monitoring or tethering. A recent study of Michigan jails showed that more than 90 percent of jail beds were maximum security while less than 9 percent of the jail population is classified as maximum security. Fifty-seven percent were medium security with the remaining 34 percent being minimum custody. More than 25 percent of those minimum-custody offenders are being housed in maximum-security beds. That is not cost-effective. Unfortunately, this scenario is not unique to Michigan.

Many of the minimum-custody cases are in jail as a condition of probation, for failure to pay child support, or for drunk driving. They could just as easily be supervised at home through the use of electronic monitoring. If at home, they could work and earn the necessary dollars to meet their financial obligations and/or do community service work. When not working, they are restricted to their residence. The technology is there that will let you know if the offender leaves his or her residence when not authorized. A new system on the market allows the officer to call the offender at home and have him or her take a Breathalyzer test. The test results, along with a picture of the offender performing the test, are recorded by a video camera in the telephone and transmitted to the parole or probation office.

Michigan's experience shows the cost to be about $11.30 a day; that includes the cost of the equipment, telephone charges, and staff to supervise the offenders and monitor the system on a twenty-four hour basis. Again, these costs are significantly less than keeping someone in jail or prison.

During the first three months of 1990, Michigan had 3,412 offenders on electronic monitoring. For the most part, these were felony offender probationers, inmates, or parolees living in the community. During that time, Michigan experienced an escape rate of 2.2 percent and had a 1.5 percent arrest rate for new felonies.

Law enforcers are frequently critical of electronic monitoring, citing the fact that offenders can drink or use drugs while home. However, offenders can do the same in jail with home brew and smuggled drugs. They also say offenders can commit new offenses while on electronic monitoring and correctional staff would not know it. That is true, but by the application of strict curfews and rigid enforcement of the conditions of supervision, along with swift and sure responses to violations, we can minimize the risk. With electronic monitoring, we can free up jail space for those offenders who pose a threat to the community.

The options this paper has just covered—shock incarceration or boot camps, intensive supervision, and electronic monitoring—are all cost-effective alternatives to prison or jail. We in corrections also must ensure that alternatives we use are high-quality, credible programs. Too often, we come up with good ideas but have failed to effectively market them and have failed to maintain credibility in our haste to expand programs to our ever-growing corrections population. We cannot build our way out of crowding, but we can overcome it by our use of cost-effective, high quality, credible programs.

2

Community Corrections— The Major Agenda Item for the Nineties

Gail D. Hughes

Deputy Director
Missouri Department of Corrections
Jefferson City, Missouri

It is the best of times, it is the worst of times—it is community corrections in the nineties. Some will say it was during the late sixties or early seventies that community corrections had its "day in the sun." Twenty-five years ago, money from the Safe Streets Act made the living easy and the good times roll. If you had an idea, there was usually a way to get some funding to try it out. However, as is usually the case in federally funded programs, the life span was short compared to the problems that corrections was facing then and now. As the federal funding faded, corrections was faced in the midseventies with Bob Martinson's articles telling us that "nothing works."

The eighties started with the first version of "read my lips" called Proposition 13 in California and the Hancock Amendment in Missouri. This legislation called for limits on government spending. Correctional agencies nationwide were hit particularly hard. Then came the Rand Corporation with its report that made many question the worth of probation. As if all this was not enough, the last half of the decade saw the demand for community corrections increasing while corrections dollars were being directed towards construction and operation of prisons to take care of an expanding institutional population. In the nineties there is no let up in prison growth. Society has become more punitive. Being hard on crime has been the call for most political campaigns.

Developing a New Strategy

Does the future look any different? This author would say "yes;" community corrections is heading for the most challenging and exciting time in its history. It is faced with managing a population in the community that the country can no longer afford to manage in prison.

Some community corrections practitioners feel they should not be in the business of managing the crowding problem. To embrace this philosophy is to put your head in the sand. Corrections professionals in both field and institutional services have the same mandate of managing convicted offenders—whatever their level of supervision or custody. The only solution to managing this tremendous overload problem lies with community corrections. Professionals in this field must take the leadership role in developing an appropriate new strategy to deal with this problem. Community corrections needs to be the centerpiece of the developing strategy. While a national strategy may be needed, even the most optimistic would agree that this is impossible. A local strategy, meaning county and city governments, does not really address the major issue unless it is combined as part of an overall state plan. Therefore, a state strategy to deal with the management of convicted felons has the most promise. Those states that have local systems as opposed to statewide systems will face a greater problem in this coordination, but these states still need to develop such a strategy.

Of over four million adults under the supervision or custody of corrections, three out of four live in the community. Community corrections is overwhelmingly the sanction of choice. The percentage who are incarcerated (25 percent) must be reduced. Many of those incarcerated are serving sentences for drug offenses or nonviolent crimes. We cannot be victimized twice, once by the crime itself, and again by the money being drained from other socially valuable programs to build and operate prisons. It is a relatively few high-profile violent offenders who have caused society to worry for its safety. In the effort to make everyone feel safe, we are incarcerating a group of offenders with no real impact on our physical safety.

Community Corrections as a Catalyst

Community corrections professionals should act as a catalyst to bring this state strategy into focus. It is essential that we bring four major groups together: parole boards, courts, institutional administrators, and community corrections. While each plays its individual role, to accomplish what is needed, these four must act in concert. The strategy must be to see that groups of convicted felons who are now incarcerated can be placed safely in the community.

Too many property offenders (including drug offenders) are being incarcerated and for too long. Also, technical probation and parole violators should not have their status revoked and take up valuable prison bed space. This author is not saying never incarcerate, never revoke and send to prison, but we should not send to prison individuals because we are angry, we lack tolerance, or we are just "tired of messing" with them. We should try—try and try again. We should assure ourselves that we exhaust every possible community alternative before we seek incarceration. The two major players that can make this happen are the courts and the parole boards. Discretionary parole release by parole boards has fallen from 72 percent in 1977 to 40 percent in 1990. However, the board's role in the management of a state's offender population is still very important. The decisions of the courts and parole boards are influenced greatly by community pressure; similarly, the legislative branch of government thinks it is expedient to be hard on crime.

Judges as well as parole boards will use community corrections in a more expansive way when they are confident that the agency offering supervision has the services available to meet the needs of clients and assure reasonable public safety. Community programs that are developed by probation and parole agencies never go wanting for clients. Usually, the programs are too small to handle the volume of work that courts and parole boards thrust on them.

Courts have filled up prison bed space, and parole boards have been reluctant to release offenders because the programs needed to make them feel comfortable with their releasing decisions have not been present. A strategy developed with all the users in mind is much more likely to establish the variety of services that are needed. We also must determine what makes the victim as well as what makes the average citizen feel comfortable with leaving convicted felons in the community. We must generate the same vigor for developing community corrections programs as we have for building prisons.

Programs with the Most Promise

The programs that may generate the most acceptance are those that have sanctions which are graduated and are highly visible to the public. This author recommends a matrix of sanctions within which individuals move depending on their progress, the seriousness of the crime, public risk, and compliance with the condition of release. This would call for a much bigger choice in alternatives than minimum and maximum field supervision. The variety of community alternatives should equal those of the most complex prison systems, from the diagnostic center to a variety of multiple-level custody institutions. For example, individuals who have violated the conditions of their probation or parole would move up and down the multiple level of sanctions based on their success at each level. Incarceration would be the last alternative, and then only for a short period of time.

Corrections should move away from large prison construction toward increased expenditures for community corrections. This does not mean a moratorium on prison construction, but prisons should only be built for the long-term, very dangerous offender. As part of the total expenditure for community corrections, we should build minimum-security, short-term (90- to 120-day, program-specific) facilities. These could be constructed near current prisons so they could have the support of basic services within population centers. These program-specific facilities would offer a new dimension to community sentence alternatives. They could be operated by community service agencies, prison authorities, or a combination of both.

These short-term facilities would add another alternative to the courts and parole board for nonviolent offenders and technical violators. Individuals would move from these short-term facilities back to the community through the sanction matrix, either to a halfway house, house arrest, intensive supervision, or back up the scale, depending on their success. This advocates the try—try again approach. If one ninety-day term in one of these facilities does not work, let us have another.

The decision is going to be made before the decade ends as to whether our course of action will be to build hundreds of prisons across this country or try another approach. Building prisons does have a seductive appeal to many outside and within corrections. However, many others strongly urge that another course of action be taken with community corrections at its forefront, a course of action that places community alternatives on the agenda of every state in this nation. This course of action should include a strategy that allows more offenders now being locked up to stay in their community; and when incarnation is the alternative it should be of short duration. Is this wishful thinking? Does it have any possibility of success? Will the new century be the best of times or the worst of times? The leadership in community corrections must answer these questions. It is their choice.

3

Leadership and Community Corrections

John J. Larivee

Executive Director
Crime and Justice Foundation
Boston, Massachusetts
President, International Community Corrections Association

Often, in public debates, community corrections positions itself as a cheaper version of the prison cell. It goes to great lengths to satisfy the popular demands that offenders on parole and probation be "incarcerated" and punished through tight surveillance and stringent restrictions on liberty. It struggles to make the case that community corrections can punish and contain offenders as well as prison, but at less cost.

Driving this is the politicization of crime and criminal justice. Public officials believe that all the public wants is a "tough" approach to crime, and that it will not tolerate risk or anything that suggests "coddling." Seeking to satisfy these controlling and punitive interests, community corrections steps away from much of its origins and much of its strength, treatment and rehabilitation, and contributes to both the perception and the reality that "nothing works."

Fearing the perception of being "soft on crime," community corrections programs avoid publicly advertising services such as substance abuse services, education and training programs, and other treatment options. Descriptions of such services are conspicuously absent from legislative testimony, community speaking engagements, and other public relations efforts describing community corrections' mission and operations. Instead, community corrections officials highlight intensive surveillance assisted by the latest technology, and emphasize punishment through forced labor and restrictions on liberty.

In addition to being excluded from marketing efforts, treatment services are being diminished in community corrections. Many officials view community corrections' responsibility as ending at "providing opportunities" for treatment. The emphasis is on coordinating services, making referrals and monitoring participation. Less concern is given to outcome. Poor performance and low achievement in treatment programs is seen to be the fault of clients who do not take advantage of these opportunities.

A Fair and Measurable Return

Public opinion surveys consistently find that citizens look to corrections and criminal justice for three goals—public safety, offender accountability, and rehabilitation. If the benefits of criminal justice investments are measured only in terms of the first two goals, public safety and offender accountability, community corrections can take the easy path by avoiding all risky offenders, and by including healthy portions of "nastiness."

However, is that all that should be expected from community corrections? Should not the community receive something more in return? Should it be content to limit the demand on corrections to "no risk and no failure?" Should not the community expect, as a fair and measurable return, that offenders become better prepared to lead law-abiding lives in the community?

Such expectations are not unreasonable. Community corrections professionals are finding value in treatment services and that particular interventions are effective in changing certain offenders. They are finding that quality treatment services—and not the intensity of control or the amount of punishment— can positively affect offenders and reduce future crime.

Herein lies both the benefit and drawback of community programs for community corrections. The benefit is making a valuable contribution to community safety by effectively changing offenders' behavior. The drawback, if viewed as such, is taking risks.

The Massachusetts Experience

What occurred in the Massachusetts prison system's community reintegration program exemplifies the disadvantages. In 1972, the Department of Correction established a reintegration program that included furloughs, prerelease centers, and other measures geared to maintain, to establish or to reestablish general societal links such as family, economic, political, and social roles. The intent was not to coddle criminals but to create better members of the community. That was achieved. The Department found a consistent reduction in future crime for inmates participating in these reintegrative services.

Between 1972 and 1987—the first fifteen years of the furlough program— more than 121,000 furloughs were granted to more than 10,000 inmates. Research found significantly lower rates of recidivism for furlough participants than for nonparticipants and that the use of the community furlough program during the period of incarceration provided a positive reintegration function. In addition, the program had a nearly flawless record—99.5 percent of the 121,000 furloughs resulted in the inmate returning to the institution without incident.

There was a similar growth in the number of inmates who participated in prerelease programming prior to parole or discharge. Between 1972 and 1987, the percentage of inmates released from the prison system who left via the prerelease program grew from 1 to 47 percent. Each year, the recidivism of those inmates was half that of inmates who did not participate in prerelease. The Department of Correction concluded that individuals who completed the prerelease programs had significantly lower rates of recidivism. While certainly no panacea to the problems of crime, these programs provided a fair and measurable return on the state's investment in its corrections system.

In 1987, one of the 0.5 percent of the furlough escapees was an inmate named Willie Horton. His brutal crimes while on furlough derailed the careers of several corrections professionals and sped up the erosion of community corrections programming, both locally and nationally. More importantly, the objective of developing better members of the community through the reintegration program was replaced by one of "no risk, no failure."

Today, Massachusetts' prison system holds 9,500 inmates. There is no furlough program; it was ended administratively in 1992. Less than 4 percent of the inmates participate in prerelease programming. Only 38 percent are paroled. In a parole system touting a 92 percent success rate, 40 percent of the inmates requesting consideration are denied, and 22 percent waive their right to a hearing. The system's goal now is no risk, no failure. It is a system that operates under the fear that an offender will falter, and the subsequent fallout will take down a department or a corrections professional.

Is the community better off with a tightened system? What is the fair and measurable return to community safety from this "get tough" investment? Do the documented results of effective community reintegration programs and treatment options influence public policy discussions? What course is advised by correctional leadership?

Unfortunately, there seems to be a rush to more incarceration and to follow more restrictive policy. Albert Einstein once defined insanity as doing the same thing over and over and expecting different results. Are we to continue touting more of the same, while expecting different results?

There will be no benefits from community programs which gauge success by the lack of failure and are managed for the lack of risk. There will be little benefit to public safety if community corrections does not provide leadership and vision. Without leadership, without clear vision of the goals and purpose of corrections, the system will continue to be buffeted by outside forces.

Corrections professionals can benefit from recognized leadership that is attentive to public opinion but not captured by it. Community corrections needs leadership that is able to speak with authority and that is willing to take responsibility for results and is not satisfied with simply "providing opportunities."

The Five Tenets of Effective Community Corrections

Dennis S. Schrantz

Strategic Planner
Wayne County Department of Community Justice
Detroit, Michigan

State and county governments throughout the United States are facing incredible budget shortfalls as a result of decreasing revenue and spiraling budgets in many areas of government. Corrections' costs are one of the main contributors to budget shortfalls as the public perception of crime, driven by increased media attention[1] tends to demand harsher, more punitive, and more expensive sentences; consequently, state legislatures often react with more ineffective mandatory sentencing laws.[2] However, intermediate sanctions, if properly designed, show promise of being more cost effective, with greater payback to the public without additional risk to public safety.[3]

One way to implement intermediate sanctions on a statewide basis is through passage of community corrections legislation. Over twenty states have passed "community corrections acts," which formulate a policy embracing "state/local partnerships" to address statewide correctional problems at the local level through creative improvement of local criminal justice systems.

Generally, community corrections acts and/or local policies prohibit the enrollment of violent criminals, a prohibition with only limited impact because the vast majority of offenders are nonassaultive. Although each state has unique attributes, all share certain commonalities: a focus on planning at the local level, collaboration with stakeholders at the state level, and citizen participation.

The Michigan Community Corrections Act of 1988 has enjoyed unprecedented participation (seventy-nine of eighty-three counties are participating to some degree), in large part because the architects of the plan created a set of principles that clearly define the relationship between state and local governments. Five basic principles or tenets of community corrections form the backbone of the state and local partnership in Michigan and may be applicable to other states. The partnership emphasizes decentralization; it links jail and prison crowding; it encourages fiscal responsibility; it employs policy-driven and data-informed decision making; and it emphasizes public education.

After five years, the impact of the Act in Michigan is clear. The prison admission rate is decreasing (from 30 percent in 1991 to 22 percent 1995) while combinations of jail and community sanctions and services are increasing.[4] While this impact has mitigated the prison crowding problem in Michigan, it has not eliminated it. Longer sentences (due at least in part to presumptive and mandatory sentences), a decrease in parole, and an increase in probation violators sentenced to prison keep population growing. However, it is impossible to deny the widespread positive impact of the community corrections act on the prison problem. This impact is due to following the five simple principles developed through a unique collaboration between the legislature and local units of government.

Decentralization

For community corrections to be effective, state governments must commit to a decentralized approach to criminal justice policymaking and program implementation. This entails not only the responsibility for setting rational policy and the programming that is required to adhere to those policies, but also including the authority to institute the policies and administer the programs.

Although a decentralized approach giving local units of government responsibility and authority is vital for community corrections, the state must provide guidelines for policy development and program implementation. The state, through its legislative and executive branches, must articulate its goal for community corrections. These goals will dictate how counties administer community corrections programs. For example, a goal of reducing prison and jail crowding would be approached much differently than a goal of expanding correctional options. In Michigan, the goal of the Community Corrections Act is to reduce admissions to prison and improve the use of local jails, consistent with public safety.

Linking Jail and Prison Crowding

If community corrections' legislation seeks to reduce reliance on a state's prison system as a response to crime, then it must recognize that prison and jail crowding are inextricably linked. Most states experiencing prison crowding can see this linkage to crowding in local jails. With no room to incarcerate locally, county justice systems send felons to state prisons.

Therefore, in Michigan, it was clear that in order for county governments to be responsive to the state problem of prison crowding, the state had to assist the counties in addressing the same problem in their local jails. Thus, the Act's goals included better use of local jails leading to reduced admissions to prison. Locally designed, comprehensive corrections plans have policies and programs to relieve pressures on the jail, including pretrial release options; in-house jail programs, which result in shorter length of stays; and community-based options such as residential drug treatment. When successful, these approaches open local jail beds for more serious felons who increasingly have been sent to the state prisons. The state offers further encouragement through a "jail reimbursement program," which provides funding to jails that house long-term felons whose sentencing guideline minimums are twelve months or more.

However, linking jail and prison crowding is only one facet of a phenomenon in the criminal justice system that might be called "system crowding." Courts, probation offices, public defenders' offices, prosecutors, and police agencies are crowded with more offenders than they can handle efficiently. Looking at a prison-crowding problem or, for that matter, a jail-crowding problem, outside of the context of "system crowding" is short sighted.

Fiscal Responsibility

For new correctional policy to be formulated and enacted at the local level, time and energy must be spent on planning. Generally, counties are not equipped to perform sophisticated analysis of the criminal justice system without technical assistance in the form of monies for county staff or consultants to collect data and examine how local systems work and to review the types and numbers of offenders in the system. This critical information is needed to perform proper planning for the policies, and programs must be driven by factual information. With the cost of incarceration ranging from $12,000 to $20,000 annually for jail inmates, and $24,000 to $56,000 for state prison inmates, counties that agree to divert offenders into local sanctions and services should expect compensation from the state. It costs money to initiate and manage intermediate sanction programs, particularly if these programs are part of a larger effort to achieve specific policy objectives that require ongoing monitoring. In addition, when an offender is diverted from a jail or prison cell, overburdened local and state probation offices have increased workloads. These constitute the ancillary costs of community corrections that must be addressed by state executive and legislative bodies through fiscal policy.

Policy-driven, Data-informed Decision Making

Criminal justice planners must avoid the tendency of criminal justice and government officials to focus solely on programs and ignore policies. The first thing planners should do is to determine the type of information that is needed to develop sound policies. Making policy decisions without adequate data will result in unsound management practices. Too often, we see "programs" as the response to jail and prison crowding and other criminal justice system problems, without adequate attention given to the formulation of overarching policies and goals that control who gets into programs and why.

Criminal justice reforms run the risk of failure when community corrections initiatives inadvertently "widen the net." This happens when offenders who otherwise would have been put on probation are placed in alternative programs where they are monitored closely. Because of this increased scrutiny, offenders in alternative programs are more likely to be caught for any violations than if they were on standard probation. When this happens, the goals of the alternatives are turned on their head as they become the cause of increasing admissions to prison.

To avoid this, criminal justice planners should follow a rational planning process that includes clear-cut goals and policies (formal agreements to a plan of action) to achieve those goals, specific objectives, and thorough "targeting." Targeting is making certain that only the persons who otherwise would be sent to jail or prison are diverted to alternative programs. Proper targeting begins with the collection of data that, when analyzed, clearly identifies how the target population is different from all others. For example, the number of prior convictions, the current charges, the probation status of an offender and when he or she committed the crime can be used as the basis for program eligibility.

Criminal justice planners must use data to create stringent eligibility criteria to protect the integrity of the programs by avoiding the phenomenon of widening the net. In addition, this data analysis should be used in the development of offender-specific approaches to the reduction of crime and recidivism. For example, in Michigan, communities that initially envisioned the development of programs for hardcore drug users changed their plans when reviewing data indicating that the primary addiction of the target population was alcohol. Communities changed their view on the level of intrusiveness needed for diverted jail inmates when they saw data indicating that the inmates were low risk.

In Michigan, the state legislature initially envisioned limiting the community corrections programs to felons whose sentencing guidelines were in the zero to twelve-month range. However, based on a review of the data regarding prison admissions, the State Community Corrections Board, appointed by the Governor to oversee the implementation of the Act, increased the target population to offenders within the zero to twenty-four month range. Moreover, the Board enacted a policy which mandated that each community develop its own targeting criteria. It is this policy which is most critical to the prison admission rate reduction in Michigan.

This approach requires sophistication in the way jurisdictions collect, analyze, and report data. But it is time well spent. Simply put, the criminal justice system must be prepared for the twenty-first century. Technology now exists for ongoing data-collection analysis that can help policymakers determine whether their approaches are working or need to be modified. Evaluations that measure the impact of community corrections must be put into place when policies are initiated. Also needed is a system to evaluate the process of how the policies and programs are being implemented (see shaded box on the next page).

In Michigan in 1990, the state launched an aggressive approach to improve data systems at three levels to better evaluate new initiatives: (1) the probation/prison admissions data system, (2) the jail data system, and (3) the community corrections program data system. These three systems allow the state to measure the impact of the new initiative and the long-term effect on recidivism.

Public Education

States that enact community corrections' legislation should inform the public about the goals, objectives, and potential benefits of such an approach. Politicians who engage in "get tough" rhetoric without addressing the costs do the public a disservice. Recent studies indicate that once the general public fully understands the costs associated with incarceration and the potential for diverting motivated offenders into more productive sanctions, they tend to support community-based programs.[5]

In Michigan, it was only when elected and government officials became aware of the public support of a full range of sanctions that they became willing to support and fully fund these efforts. Michigan developed a "strategic public education campaign" that informed the public, community by community, about the benefits of the Community Corrections Act. As a result, the media increased favorable coverage of community-based programs from an average of eight articles a month to over thirty per month statewide.[6]

The message must be clear and strong: There are safe, effective ways to punish and rehabilitate offenders without putting them behind bars.

The Development of Intermediate Sanctions Through a Policy-driven, Data-informed, Decision Making Process

Policy	What is the goal?
	What are the values driving the goal?
Outcome	What specific, measurable, objectives do you desire?
Target	What offender population do you need to isolate to achieve your outcome/objective goal?
Characteristics/ Profiles	What characteristics make this target population different from the population you wish to avoid?
Services/Sanctions	What services and sanctions are needed to affect behavior change, based on these characteristics; what program designs are needed to offer these services and sanctions to the target group?
System Analysis	What is the timing of decisions; what are the mechanisms by which decisions are made? Who are the decision makers? How do these variables need to be harnessed to meet the goals and objectives; in other words, what is the implementation policy?
Implementation Plan	Who will do what and when to get the job done?

Notes:

[1] See "Crime Down, Media Crime Coverage Up" from Media Monitor as reported by *Overcrowded Times*, April, 1994.

[2] See, for example, "Evaluating Mandatory Minimums" by Walter Dickey, *Overcrowded Times*, December, 1993.

[3] See, for example, the working papers from the November 1993 national conference: "What Works in Community Corrections: A Consensus Conference" sponsored by the International Association of Residential and Community Alternatives (IARCA).

[4] See, Biannual Report to the Michigan Legislature; Measuring the Impact of Public Act 511; Michigan Office of Community Corrections; March, 1995.

[5] See, for example, Crime and Punishment: The Public's View; A Quantitative Analysis of Public Opinion, by the Public Agenda Foundation for the Edna McConnell Clark Foundation; John Doble; June, 1987.

[6] See Educating the Public About Community Corrections; Public Education Plan, Public Information Office; Michigan Office of Community Corrections; August, 1991.

Optimal Conditions for Community Corrections

Roger Lauen, Ph.D.

Private consultant
Seattle, Washington

Brad Bogue, MA, CAC III

Project director
Colorado Standardized Offender Assessment Program
Office of Probation Services
State Court Administrator's Office
Denver, Colorado

Introduction

As the demand for more jail and prison cells increased, there was a parallel demand for alternatives to incarceration, sometimes referred to as intermediate sanctions or more generically as community corrections. Examples of intermediate sanctions programs include: many forms of intensive supervision programs under auspices of probation, electronic monitoring, and home confinement oftentimes as a condition of probation, residential and nonresidential community corrections programs, boot camps, day treatment centers, and similar intensive supervision programs under parole auspices. All of these intermediate sanction programs were developed in the context of a very politically conservative era (late 1970s to early 1990s). Evidence of this ideological conservatism is found in the names of the programs themselves: community punishment programs. In the mid-1990s, a state of confusion exists. The "get tough" rhetoric is resonating with an emerging revival of rehabilitation in many corrections' systems.

Intermediate sanctions is a dual-edged sword. One edge is that intermediate sanctions programs are less expensive, divert offenders from jail or prison, provide a community context within which appropriate treatment services can be delivered, offer an opportunity for offenders to get connected (or reconnected) to community resources, and, if done correctly, can reduce recidivism. The other edge of intermediate sanctions programs is that they increase correctional costs because they widen the net of social control (they serve offenders who would, in the absence of intermediate sanctions, be served by a less expensive correctional option, such as normal probation), they increase crowding because offenders in intermediate sanctions programs have high rates of technical rule violations and, as a result, are placed in jail or prison, and they are unidimensional in that they focus almost exclusively on surveillance.

The research literature is quite clear about the impact of intermediate sanctions programs since 1980:

- Correctional costs have increased considerably. Most of this increase in correctional spending was not money well spent. The unidimensional approach, emphasizing risk and more correctional control, resulted in a significant increase in technical rule violations, violations of probation and parole orders, and some increase in new offenses.
- The performance of offenders on intermediate sanctions programs, as measured by recidivism, was no better or worse than placing the same offenders on less intense (regular probation/parole) supervision programs (Petersilia and Turner 1993; Cullen, Wright, and Applegate 1996).

There is, on the other hand, an emerging vision for intermediate sanctions programs equally supported by research, that offers more hope. What follows is a brief and broad summary of particular conditions or elements that contribute to the positive side of intermediate sanctions. These conditions are organized into seven domains of community corrections with which most practitioners should be reasonably familiar:

1. Theory
2. Political policy, policymaker and media
3. Organizational setting
4. Correctional staff
5. Programming
6. Community
7. Offender

1. Theory

Many correctional practitioners are insufficiently informed about trends and developments regarding theories of criminal behavior. Earlier theoretical notions such as strain, social disorganization, labeling, and so on, tended to be monolithic conceptualizations of societal processes and as such, they did not lend themselves to operating within corrections. More recently, the field of criminology has been involved in aggressive integration of old and new ideas, cross-discipline evaluations, and a trend toward more shifting between analysis of large scale phenomena (such as social class of the offender) and analysis of small scale phenomena (such as attitudes of the offender). All of this has eroded many so-called barriers between applied and basic science, affording improved and more relevant theories for corrections.

While the pursuit of integrated theories is the trend in criminology today, social learning theories (based on Sutherland's differential association theory) appear to dominate. Social scientists now can explain slightly over half the variance in criminal behavior. Social learning propositions now account for approximately 80 percent of that explained variance.

The more community corrections and intermediate sanctions programs operate on the basis of social learning principles, the more likely it is that they will be effective in reducing criminal conduct. The basic idea of social learning theory is that criminal activities are learned, just as law-abiding behavior is learned. Given this, with the appropriate support, practice, and reinforcement, criminal behaviors can be unlearned, and a prosocial lifestyle can take their place. Hence, the guiding theoretical principles behind risk and needs assessment is social learning theory. A theory specifically tailored to adult offenders is the psychology of criminal conduct developed by the Ottawa School (Andrews and Bonta 1994; Palmer 1992; Lipsey and Wilson 1993).

2. The Political Arena: Policy Making, Policymakers, and the Media.

Corrections' policy is made by a variety of people and influenced by many organizational interests. One group that has a profound role in shaping corrections' policy is public and elected officials, working in conjunction with print and TV media. This coalition of public officials and private media works in approximately the same way from state to state. An elected official amplifies the emotionally "hot" rhetoric surrounding a heinous crime. The official expresses moral outrage, sorrow for the victim(s), and promises retribution and severe punishment for the offender. The retribution is formulated in terms of more severe criminal sanctions: mandatory prison time, longer prison terms, and life without parole.

The correctional consequences of this syndrome are evident: jail and prison populations have doubled in the past decade. Quite unexpectedly, community corrections populations also doubled during the same period. Additionally, county commissioners have been forced to realign county priorities as jail construction and operating costs have soared. Probation caseloads, which already were unwieldy, became so large and unmanageable that large segments of the caseload were simply ignored, turned over to volunteers, or given a fistful of postcards and told to "check in" occasionally. This correctional gridlock was not anticipated and certainly not a part of the political script of the "get tough" crowd in the early and middle 1980s.

The relationship between elected officials, the media, crime victims, and others is a symbiotic one. Legislation is written by crime victim representatives and local prosecutors, and in some cases (such as in California) by correctional officer unions. Elected officials presenting themselves as crime fighters win election and reelection on unidimensional "get tough" political platforms.

The TV media, operating on opinion polling information and marketing advice on the emotional power of violent crime, present the public with a highly distorted picture of crime. In reality, violent crime constitutes a small slice (about 10 percent nationally) of all serious index crimes reported to police. Yet, TV media present violent crime almost exclusively. Further, crime stories make up an increasing proportion of all news (Media Monitor 1995; Frankel 1995).

This purposeful distortion of crime meets the publicity needs of crime victims, correctional officers, private prison promoters, and financial investment and municipal bond firms. It also provides economic development for small town advocates, and of course, it helps the elected officials playing the "get tough" card.

The general public and corrections practitioners first must understand that there is such a coalition and then attempt to break up, interject, interrupt, or somehow provide this coalition with a different perspective. This different view should include basic crime facts such as: nonviolent crime is on the downswing, violent crime is increasing slightly in spite of a quadrupling of incarceration since 1980, and violent crime is a small part of a much larger, more complex crime phenomenon. Further, crime prevention and crime fighting techniques must match the complexity of crime causation and not be reduced to slogneering and simplistic sound bites such as "three strikes and you're out."

3. Organizational Conditions

Corrections organizations are quite traditional. Most are top down, hierarchical organizations. A better way to go, a way that allows and encourages new ideas, is a flat organizational structure. In a flat organization, salary, authority, and skills are on a more egalitarian basis. A one-to-three or one-to-four wage ratio between line staff and the director is a good place to start. Such an organization should have a reward system that places high value on competency and includes literacy in crime theory, risk variables associated with criminal behavior, and risk and needs assessment. The organization should have experience working with offenders and provide training in current correctional intervention techniques (including cognitive skill-building curriculums, motivational interviewing, preventing relapse, and matching the offender with a change strategy that is acceptable and appropriate). Finally, the organization should have a professional commitment to excellence in correctional practice.

The initiative for internal program controls, sound management information systems, and on-going operational process/performance measures (staff, program services, key case management functions) should come from the program itself and not depend on pressures of people or groups outside the program (even though local and state agencies almost always have reporting requirements of their own).

4. Staff

When possible, it is preferable and easier to hire "smart" rather than attempt to train "smart." Many very talented, well-educated, highly motivated college graduates are applying for jobs in corrections. These recent college graduates often are already familiar with both tested theories and new technologies, have adequate specialized training, and are capable of handling entry-level responsibilities in the corrections field. Conversely, it is a much bigger challenge (more time consuming and more expensive) to retrain correctional practitioners who have been on the job for many years. Whether new graduates or old employees, correctional practitioners should be knowledgeable in crime theories, assessment techniques that can isolate risk and criminogenic needs, and a wide range of correctional interventions that can be tailored to the individual offender's treatment needs.

A community corrections program should incorporate a diversity of skills, backgrounds, and philosophies. In this regard, more is better. For example, some staff should have extensive experience and knowledge in substance abuse treatment theory and practice. Other staff should know the local labor market, have a working relationship with local employers, know how to get offenders enrolled in vocational training schools, and have experience in placing and supporting offenders on the job. Still other staff must be competent in applied social science and be able to improve the internal evaluation system, upgrade the forms and assessment tools, and revise the program's theoretical base when new theories are introduced or old ones revised.

Staff competencies might best be viewed in three distinct but interwoven tiers.

- Tier One is the moral/ethical or honorable person dimension. The desired attributes of this tier are honesty, reliability, an ability to focus on the offender's supervision and treatment needs, and a communication's style that is firm, fair, and empathetic. From a social learning perspective, sufficient modeling of prosocial norms and behavior is a critical dynamic that should not be taken for granted.

- Tier Two is a centuries-old concept of apprentice-journeyperson-master. This concept recognizes that staff skills are differentiated and measurable and that time plays an important part in perfecting one's craft. For example, apprentices will have clearly defined jobs (security and line staff, front desk) and must acquire specific measurable skills to be promoted to the journeyman/woman class. Journeymen/women will likewise have distinct roles (case manager, line staff supervisor) and will not move to the master class until master class level skills (certificates and competency tests in essential legal parameters, relapse prevention, motivational interviewing, assessment, cognitive skills training, social learning theory, case planning and computer literacy) have been attained. Master class staff are the staff trainers, program directors and liaisons with outside agencies.

• Tier Three has nothing to do with acquiring skills but is a matching of staff skills and characteristics with the criminogenic needs and characteristics of the offender population. Higher energy staff are preferable for operating cognitive skill-building groups. Another obvious example would be to hire experienced Afro-American and Latino women when the offender population largely is female minorities.

All staff should have the ability to communicate orally and in writing (sometimes in two languages) with offenders, each other, with judges, prosecutors, defense attorneys, the public, potential employers, and other allied human service agencies. The easiest, but by no means a foolproof method, is to require all staff to have a college degree.

Community corrections staff should view the surrounding community as a resource, not the enemy. Offenders are in intermediate sanctions or community corrections programs for only a brief time, but live in the community for many years. The thirty-year-old concept of community corrections staff as a broker of community resources is a valid and useful notion. However, staff must have a working knowledge of existing agencies and services in the surrounding community and develop interagency agreements for referrals, interagency staff training, and cooperative proposal and funding arrangements. The staff's job is to function as an advocate and agent on behalf of the offender with other community agencies.

5. Program

All programs should be committed to changing offenders' behavior. The correctional intervention literature now provides practitioners not just hope that treatment is beneficial, but specific tools and direction about how that intervention can be applied with which type of offender. Lipsey, Palmer, Bonta, Andrews, and Gendreau and others have assembled a fairly significant knowledge base; all we have to do is read it.

The first and perhaps the most important task of any program is to conduct a careful assessment of the offender's risk, criminogenic needs, and potential responsiveness to various treatment approaches. Offender risk/need instruments have evolved through several generations of technology, and many current assessment tools with varying psychometric properties are now available. The Level of Supervision Inventory (LSI), an offender assessment instrument developed in Canada that has recently become popular in many parts of the United States, represents a breed of more versatile assessment tools.

Assessment tools, such as the Level of Supervision Inventory, the Community Risk/Needs Management Scale, or most recently, the Compass, that integrate risk and need factors, help staff to identify not only relative risk levels but the key criminogenic need areas of one offender as opposed to another. These need areas often involve dynamic factors and can become "moving targets." Comprehensive assessment tools form the foundation from which to survey an individual's progress or regression; they also serve as the basis for linking further secondary assessments when more "fine grain" information is indicated in a particular treatment area.

While the offender is under supervision and in the program, he or she is changing. The challenge for staff is to stay in touch with the offender to know the direction and depth of these changes. In general, offenders who are periodically and immediately reinforced for their progress in acquiring prosocial skills and stability will do better than offenders without program reinforcement. Conversely, as offenders revert to abusing drugs or alcohol or criminal activities, additional surveillance and an intensification of treatment also must be immediate. This "staying in touch" can and must be done by a continual reassessment of risk and needs at given intervals.

All offenders have their own style of learning and level of motivation to change. To match offenders to specific treatment modalities intelligently— according to characteristics of the offender—is central to the responsivity principle. A number of studies indicate that treatment outcomes may be significantly enhanced by careful discrimination in fitting offenders to different types of treatment modalities. "Different strokes for different folks" should apply in terms of matching the offender with the particular supervision and treatment style of staff and the types of services offered in the larger community (Hester and Miller 1995; Palmer 1992).

6. Community

The community is the host; community corrections programs and staff are the guests. The community has resources; community corrections programs and staff are the brokers of those resources. The most important resource is local community members. Community corrections staff must meet with, cajole, and attempt to persuade community members to mobilize on behalf of offenders. Most communities have retired craftspeople such as artists, electricians, truck drivers, cooks, plumbers, teachers, and carpenters. If approached correctly, many retired people would welcome the opportunity to give a few hours a week to assist community corrections clients.

Two examples of programs that have used volunteers extensively and effectively are the Community Corrections Council in Morristown, New Jersey, and the county jail in Springfield, Massachusetts. Volunteers must be trained and assigned tasks that are consistent with their interests and skills. Plumbers, electricians, and carpenters can provide on-site preconstruction skills training as well as on-the-job monitoring of offenders' work performance. Educators, artists, and counselors can assist with Adult Basic Education and GED training.

All community corrections programs, including probation and parole, should have a board of directors. The board should be made up of community volunteers. When community volunteers are board members, they become stakeholders and develop a sense of ownership in correctional programs. They take a more personal interest in the offender, and the offender's performance is seen the same way a stockholder views a profit and loss statement. As board members, community volunteers do not just "help out," they begin to mobilize their expertise, skills, and resources in the same way they do for a friend or family member.

Another example of the use of volunteers is a private industry council (PIC). Private industry councils were developed and used by United States Department of Labor programs in the late 1970s and 1980s. A private industry council is made up of private employers, public labor officials, and private and public vocational, education, and training officials. The objective is to organize both the public, but especially the private sector, on behalf of the employment needs of offenders. Recognizing that higher-paying jobs that lead to rewarding careers go to people with informal and influential connections, the private industry council can assist offenders in ways that they cannot on their own. Like the board of directors, the private industry council provides a forum through which vocational training and job opportunities can be expedited for offenders, and it mobilizes and coordinates employment resources which are often fragmented.

Social support studies suggest that the stronger the network, and the greater the rate of support through exchange of material and informational and emotional resources, the greater the indirect (resiliency) and direct (positive self-image) effects. Community corrections programs with high rates of support exchange (between staff and offenders in the program and community members and agencies external to the program) are likely to produce greater and more sustainable positive effects.

7. Offender

In considering offenders, there are two points, so obvious they are often overlooked, that are worth mentioning. They are: (1) offenders outnumber staff, and (2) the resources of individual offenders (social support, motivation, and self-efficacies) are the most critical factor in determining treatment outcomes. Failure to recognize these simple truths results in fundamental imbalance, inefficient power struggles, and both atrophy and entropy of client-to-staff relationships. Careful attention to these points should promote cooperation and trust between offenders and staff and reduce the adversarial climate when conflict, which is inevitable, occurs.

Realistically, our scope of control over offender behaviors in the community is quite limited. A typical caseload of thirty offenders may afford the officer the luxury of demanding a given offender's "undiluted" attention for two hours out of an entire week. With electronic home monitoring and weekly drug tests, one might further restrict an offender's range of geographical activity and drug taking by 50 percent and 25 percent, respectively (assuming one is 100 percent efficient at surveilling the parameters and enforcing them). Though we may and should impact some of the offender's reinforcement system, most of each offender's behavior and activity remains under the control of the offender.

Not only can practitioners actually control very little of an offender's behavior in the community, they always incur the risk of affecting offender behavior in counterintuitive and unproductive ways. If imposed externally and without skills, some offenders resist or react when a valued liberty is threatened. These effects tend to enhance the value and attractiveness of the threatened liberties and, thus, magnify the challenge for some offenders to "beat the system."

The treatment outcome literature shows that the offenders themselves are the most critical change agent in obtaining successful outcomes. Matching and fidelity to appropriate modality significantly contribute, but only in the neighborhood of 10 percent to 20 percent of the variance. Perhaps as much as 30 percent of the variance in treatment outcomes can be explained by the style of the therapist (for example, empathetic versus confrontive). This leaves approximately half the variance as currently explained by what resources the client brings to the situation, including placebo effects. To overlook this dynamic would be inviting failure.

One successful model to insure that offender dynamic is not overlooked is called FRAMES. It is used in brief therapies and motivational interviewing. FRAMES is an acronym for a reiterative process designed to resolve offender ambivalence and optimize motivation for change. The components include:

Feedback:	provide client impartial feedback
Responsibility:	emphasize client as decision maker
Advice:	give simple suggestions with warm regard
Menu:	offer options
Empathy:	show concerned understanding
Self-efficacy:	reinforce client's self-sufficiency

Engaging the offender in this process provides a type of reality test, especially during case planning. Given these points, it is critical that practitioners learn and cultivate skills to work with offenders' energy for change. While this energy may not, at least initially, perfectly coincide with criminogenic needs that staff have prioritized, it should not be dismissed. It is much easier to steer a moving car rather than a parked car. Ultimately, a balancing dialogue is necessary between assessment-informed staff and offenders and their real motivations to achieve optimum prosocial change.

Summary

Community corrections and intermediate sanctions are part of a complex, multifaceted system. To work optimally, community corrections must be much more than a sophisticated social control strategy (with approaches such as electronic monitoring, urinalysis, and phone checks). Ideally, community corrections must start with good ideas and theories and build assessment, supervision, and treatment strategies consistent with those basic ideas and theories.

Skilled and highly committed staff can do much to change offender behavior, but without the involvement of a wide band of community members, the staff will have only a limited impact. The community itself must be mobilized to assist community corrections in its mission to guide offenders toward a new path, a prosocial lifestyle, and full membership in the host community.

References

Andrews, D. A., and James Bonta. 1994. *The Psychology of Criminal Conduct.* Cincinnati: Anderson Publishing.

Cullen, F., J. Wright, and B. Applegate. 1996. Control in the Community. In Alan Harland, ed. *Choosing Correctional Options that Work.* Newbury Park, CA: Sage Publications.

Frankel, Max. 1995. The Murder Broadcasting System. *New York Times Magazine,* December 17, 1995.

Gendreau, Paul. 1996. Offender Rehabilitation: What We Know and What Needs To Be Done. *Criminal Justice and Behavior.* (23)1: 144-161.

Hester, Reid K., and William R. Miller. 1995. *Handbook of Alcoholism Treatment Approaches,* 2nd Edition. Boston: Allyn & Bacon.

Lipsey, M., and D. Wilson. 1993. The Efficacy of Psychological, Educational, and Behavioral Treatment: Confirmation from Meta-analysis. *American Psychologist.* (48): 1181-1209.

Media Monitor. 1995. Media Crime Wave Continues: Crime Tops TV News for Second Year. *Overcrowded Times.* Vol. 6, No. 2, April, p. 5.

Palmer, T. 1992. *The Re-emergence of Correctional Intervention.* Newbury Park, CA: Sage Publications.

Petersilia, J., and S. Turner. 1993. Intensive Probation and Parole. In M. Tonry, ed. *Crime and Justice: A Review of Research.* Chicago: University of Chicago Press.

6

Probation and Parole Violators in South Carolina

Richard P. Stroker

Deputy Director for Field Services
South Carolina Department of Probation,
 Parole and Pardon Services
Columbia, South Carolina

In 1989, the South Carolina Department of Probation, Parole, and Pardon Services began to review all of its practices concerning the handling of probation and parole violators. What we learned from this review surprised and interested us, and launched us on a journey of exploration and experimentation that is still continuing. Our practices, policies, and expectations have been largely reshaped over the past seven years as we have tried to improve all aspects of our work in the area of probation and parole violations. This article will try to explain some of the things that we have learned and changed about our work in this area.

We had several motives for undertaking this review. First, we wanted to determine if our procedures worked well for our own staff. Front line staff and supervisors had been expressing some concerns about our violation procedures for some time. These concerns focused on the length of time that was devoted to each aspect of work in this area, and the total time required to resolve any particular violation. Staff also was concerned about the lack of concurrence between their violation recommendations and the outcomes imposed by the courts and the parole board. Second, we wanted to determine if our violation procedures operated in harmony with our supervision strategies. We had modified our offender supervision strategies during the 1980s, and we had embraced notions of risk management, risk-based classifications, and the use of community sentencing options based on the risk or needs that may be posed by the offender. Third, we were mindful of the impact that revoked offenders have on prisons and jails in our state. We wanted to more fully investigate our involvement in this area in light of the increasing number of offenders who were having their probation or parole revoked. Finally, we knew that our courts and parole board were operating with a heavy workload, and we wanted to make sure that we were using their time well. With a grant from the National Institute of Corrections (NIC), and considerable assistance provided by staff from the Center for Effective Public Policy and NIC, we began to pursue our interests.

Probation and parole agents of the department provide community supervision to over 40,000 criminal offenders. These offenders include all adults placed on probation or parole in South Carolina, as well as inmates released to community supervision under special programs or statutes. We have a variety of sentencing options and community alternatives that can be imposed at the time of sentencing or as a condition of parole. These include specialized residential options such as Restitution Centers, Community Control Centers (which focus on substance abuse, cognitive development, and life skills issues), home detention programs (with or without electronic monitoring), intensive supervision efforts, public service employment programs, specialized treatment programs and referrals, and many other possible sanctions. All of these sentencing options are administered by the Department of Probation, Parole, and Pardon Services. Upon the discovery of a violation, probation and parole agents have the authority, with the approval of their immediate supervisor, to issue a warrant to place the offender in custody. Once placed in custody, probationers and parolees have the ability, under state statutes, to be considered for release on bond. Ultimately, a judge (in probation cases) or the parole board would determine the disposition of the violation.

While we knew how many offenders were ultimately revoked from various supervision programs, we understood very little about what the violations were, and why any particular outcome occurred. We created a flow-chart representing our violations process, and we realized how complicated this process was. We looked at the impact that our warrants had on local jails, where offenders often would wait for a considerable period of time (if they were unable to meet bond requirements) on the disposition of their case. We began to gather data about violations and outcomes, and we were amazed to learn how seldom judges agreed with our recommendations. We talked with our agents, and found out how much of their time and energy was being wasted by our own requirements. We learned that judges and parole board members felt overwhelmed with the number of cases we were presenting. In short, we knew that we had considerable room for improvement.

Designing a Framework for Effectively Responding to Violations

We began our efforts to improve our violations system by considering our goals for the supervision of offenders. We felt that our violations system should reflect the same basic philosophies and approaches that were present in our management of offenders. We also believed that our violations practices should be harmonious with our release policies. That is, the same principles that help us determine who should be under our supervision, and how we should attempt to manage them, should drive our decisions about what to do with offenders who fail to meet our conditions.

The cornerstone of our release and supervision efforts is offender risk. We have risk instruments that help us determine the best candidates for parole, and to establish the supervision level that may be appropriate for a particular individual. Using static and dynamic variables which we validated and revalidated, we had developed some specific risk-management approaches to our work. The second ingredient present in these systems was some personal observation and knowledge concerning the activities of the offender. While our risk instruments helped us to make broad classifications, our individual observations helped us to determine the best course of individual action within the ranges of discretion that were allowed.

Finally, in the area of supervision, we allowed a considerable number of decisions to be made at the front line. The agent and his or her supervisor had the best information about an offender's situation. In this way, frontline staff could make determinations about what needed to be done in specific cases. So, in considering our approaches to supervision and release, we believed that our violation practices should reflect risk-management principles, be impacted by a personal understanding of the activities of the offender, and that decisions made at the frontline level offered the best opportunity to determine the most appropriate outcome.

In looking at practical considerations, we discovered several problems that we hoped to correct. First, acquiring a final response to violations seemed to take a long time. Often, court dockets and parole hearing schedules prevented a quick review. In many cases, the time between initial incarceration and final resolution was many months. Second, after this sometimes lengthy wait, the offender was returned to our supervision in over half of the violation cases heard. Third, jail administrators were concerned with the number of violators placed in their jails and the length of time that violators were detained in their jails waiting for a disposition. Fourth, the number of offenders who were being revoked was increasing at a rate higher than the rate of increase in supervision cases. Fifth, opinions varied between counties of our state, and sometimes even between staff in the same county, about what the most appropriate response should be to a particular set of violation circumstances. Last, we found some confusion among staff about the purpose and goals of supervision itself, with sometimes widely differing views about the responsibilities of the agent and the responsibilities of the offender.

Putting the Pieces Together

To increase consistency between staff, to create some harmony with our other areas of responsibility, and to resolve the problems that were present in our violations' practices, we decided to do six things:

1. We would encourage staff to be proactive in dealing with violations. Instead of allowing violations to pile up, we would seek out and address the reasons for and possible solutions to each violation.

2. This proactive response to violations would be coupled with a clear message concerning the purpose of supervision. Through policies, training, and other opportunities, we stressed that the purpose of supervision was to attempt to stimulate positive outcomes. To accomplish our broader supervision expectations, we needed agents to anticipate potential problems, develop appropriate case plans, and appropriately respond to violations of our conditions. By discussing supervision goals and violation responses together, we were able to better integrate two critical aspects of our work.

3. We would develop guidelines to assist staff in determining a response to particular violations. These violation guidelines would consider the seriousness of the violation and the risks posed by the offender, and would offer responses that were proportional to this severity and risk.

4. As a part of this proactive approach, we would empower staff, both line agents and departmental hearing officers, to resolve cases at their level, impose the most appropriate and least onerous sanction necessary for the situation, and allow offenders to continue in the community under modified conditions unless the severity of their violation or the individual risks posed by the offender required incarceration. This would bring speedier dispositions to many cases.

5. We would create an alternative means of moving violation cases forward that would not require a warrant and detention, but instead would operate similar to a summons.

6. We would gather information and data and modify our processes further as needed.

We initiated our new violations' procedures with parole cases and implemented them in about one-third of the counties of the state in 1989. By 1990, we extended our new procedures to parole cases in all counties of the state. In 1991, we began expanding our practices to probation cases by initially working with one judge in one county. In 1992, we expanded to additional counties. We have since expanded this process to all counties and all cases under the jurisdiction of the department.

Each time that we expanded our violations' procedures to a new area, we evaluated our information and made some adjustments where we thought they were necessary. These adjustments included expanding the authority of hearing officers and frontline staff to impose additional sanctions; allowing for certain violations to bypass the administrative hearing process and proceed directly to the court or the parole board; modifying our violations' guidelines and categories; providing greater clarity in the use of our summons; and modifying specific supervision techniques and classifications. With each expansion of our process, we provided extensive training to staff on the violations' procedures and on our expectations and purposes in making these modifications. We developed specialized training programs for frontline supervisors and for hearing officers. During all phases of the development and modification of our violations' process, we involved a significant number of staff to determine what the issues were, and what the best answers might be.

Violation Responses

The heart of our system centers on allowing staff to respond quickly and appropriately to violations by offenders. We believe that it is absolutely essential to respond to violations rapidly if we are going to have any success with influencing the behavior of the offender, with helping to generate a successful supervision outcome, and with meeting our public safety responsibilities. Our process is fairly simple. Once a violation is detected, the agent discusses the situation with his or her supervisor. The agent and supervisor determine if some sanction can be imposed at their level, thus resolving the violation matter, or if a warrant or summons (which we call a citation) should be issued. If a warrant or citation is issued, the case is heard at an administrative hearing by a departmental hearing officer. The hearing officer determines if there is probable cause to believe that a violation has been committed, and if one has been committed, the hearing officer can impose a community supervision sanction (for example, impose a home detention requirement). If the offender is unwilling to accept the sanctions that have been proposed by departmental employees, then the case is referred to the court or parole board, as appropriate, for resolution. If no community sanction is appropriate for the violation, then the matter is referred to the court or parole board, and a revocation of probation or parole is recommended.

Frontline agents and supervisors may do any of the following things immediately in response to a violation if they determine that the offender does not pose an undue risk to the community and that the violation does not constitute what we consider to be a serious violation:

- Place the offender in a nonresidential or residential treatment facility or refer the offender to an appropriate treatment provider
- Place the offender in a halfway house for up to sixty days
- Impose up to forty hours of public service employment (perform free labor for the benefit of governmental or nonprofit entities)
- Place offenders already under intensive supervision on home detention
- Reprimand the offender verbally or in writing
- Restructure the supervision plan

- Counsel the offender
- Increase drug testing
- Increase supervision reporting requirements

At the administrative hearing, any of the following sanctions may be imposed by the hearing officer:

- Place the offender on intensive supervision
- Place the offender on home detention for up to six months with or without electronic monitoring
- Order the offender to perform up to 300 hours of public service employment
- Order a residential or nonresidential placement in a treatment facility
- Exempt the payment of fees
- Order placement in the Coastal Addictions Treatment residential program
- Recommend to the court or parole board placement in the Restitution Center
- Recommend to the court or parole board placement in the Community Control Center
- Recommend to the court or parole board revocation
- Take any action that the agent could take

Results of the New Violations' Procedures

The modifications we made to the violations' system produced immediate results. Because agents were now encouraged and empowered to respond to all violations, many more violations were identified and handled. However, this did not increase the workload for jails, judges, or the parole board. In 1995, for example, many thousands of violations were handled by agents and their supervisors. About 12,000 administrative hearings were held. In these 12,000 cases, over 6,000 of these offenders had been served with citations instead of warrants, thus easing the strain on local jails. And of these 12,000 cases, nearly 7,000 resulted in the offender continuing in the community with additional sanctions imposed by the hearing officer. Because the more minor violations are screened out, courts and the parole board are not faced with as many revocation cases. Concurrence between our recommendation and the court or parole board's final action also has increased dramatically. In 1995, courts concurred with our recommendations in over 85 percent of the cases (up from about 35 percent prior to the implementation of our new procedures). The parole board concurred with our recommendation in over 95 percent of the cases. While the actual number of total offenders revoked and incarcerated in prison has increased from the number revoked in 1989, this growth reflects the increasing offender population that has been placed under our jurisdiction.

In 1989, we supervised about 28,500 probation and parole offenders and about 5 percent of this population had their supervision revoked and were incarcerated in prison as a result. This represented about 13 percent of prison admissions during the year. In 1994, we supervised slightly more that 37,000 probation and parole offenders, and again about 5 percent of our probation and parole population had their supervision revoked and were incarcerated in prison as a result. These revocations represented about 14 percent of prison admissions during that year. These figures do not include special populations such as those sentenced under the Youthful Offender Act or the supervised furlough populations that we also supervise. Thus, despite the fact that we have become much more proactive in the identification and response to violations, we have not had a disproportionate impact on prison bed spaces. And as our increase in concurrence rates demonstrates, we believe that we are doing a much better job of identifying those offenders who are appropriate for revocation.

As indicated previously, thousands of violation cases a year were diverted from court dockets by having their cases disposed of at administrative hearings. This has clearly had a positive impact on judges and court personnel. And finally, the use of citations instead of warrants in roughly half of the violation cases that could not be disposed of at the agent/supervisor level has been of some considerable benefit to local jails. This has meant that about 6,000 offenders who otherwise would have been incarcerated in a local jail while awaiting bond or some disposition to their case can now await their hearing while remaining in the community.

Lessons We Learned

These results are most encouraging. We discovered several significant problems, and we believe we have taken many positive steps to address what we have found. There are few areas more important in probation and parole work than the handling of violations. In many ways, this area is a window on the entire operation and philosophy of a supervision entity. The further we explored this area, the more we realized the need to bring greater clarity and focus to our supervision policies and procedures. As a result, we now have new supervision policies, engage in more supervision and violation training for staff, and are more conscious of the impact that we have on the other members of the criminal justice community. Studying internal violation practices is something that all probation and parole agencies should do.

On the practical side, we have seen some dramatic results. Because of our desire to respond proactively to each violation, we attend to more violations than ever before. Because most of these violations are resolved within the department at the lowest possible level, we are able to screen out thousands of cases that were previously going to the courts and the parole board. We believe that we have become more effective at accomplishing our overall supervision goal of assisting offenders to achieve a positive supervision outcome because we now do a better job of explaining our expectations to offenders, of identifying significant factors that may effect the outcome of the case, and of appropriately responding to the violations that we find. Because offenders know that we will hold them accountable for their actions, and that we are trying to work with them to produce a positive supervision outcome, we provide a framework within which agents and offenders can better understand their duties and responsibilities.

Our efforts have not come at the expense of prisons or jails. We believe that our practices have had a particularly positive impact on jail crowding issues. We have increased the consistency of our own actions as well as the concurrence between our recommendations and the court or parole board's action. We have explored and refined a variety of supervision approaches and techniques, and have become better able to identify the particular methods that we wish to use with both high-risk and lower-risk offenders.

To maximize the use of resources, we have had to do a better job of determining who needs more supervision and who needs less, and better provide what is required to both populations. To create more time and lower caseloads for agents managing higher-risk offenders, we have experimented with a variety of ways to manage large groups of offenders who pose lower risk. These methods have included the use of technology, automation, and group reporting.

We demonstrated confidence in frontline staff and supervisors and involved them in the solutions to their problems. We tried to find ways to stop wasting time and resources, and instead have modified our work in ways that will maximize our time and energies. This has had a positive impact on the attitudes and motivation of staff. We discovered variations in practices that we did not know existed. We found a lack of clarity concerning broad issues where we assumed that all was clear.

The way that we proceeded in attempting to resolve our issues—starting small and slowly adding other counties—served us well. It gave us the opportunity to work out the details and allowed for positive word-of-mouth to spread. However, we are not through with our work in this area. Perhaps we never will be. The desire to find ways to improve our efforts has stimulated a fairly constant stream of ideas and innovations.

Conclusion

Perhaps the old adage that "life is 10 percent what happens to you and 90 percent how you react to it" holds particular meaning in the area of violations. While we hope to become smarter about anticipating violations by offenders, we have to clearly understand why we respond to any particular violation in the manner that we do. Our work in this area has demonstrated the importance of several things. First is the significance of outlining our goals and expectations for supervision and harmonizing our expectations concerning the handling of violations with those concerning supervision. Second is the importance of trying to understand what we do, how we do it, and why we do it, before we go about trying to resolve anything. It was very helpful for us to spend the time necessary to involve many staff, flow-chart our system, and gather the data that was available before we attempted to go forward at all. Last, once we knew what goals we were seeking, it was critical that we provide staff the time, tools, clarity of direction, and flexibility needed to meet those goals.

It has been said that changing a policy was like trying to change tires on a moving car. Changing your entire perspective and activities associated with the violations' area is at least this hard. However, the potential rewards for staff, and for the broader criminal justice community, make it well worth the effort that is required.

7

Probation and Parole Officers: Police Officers or Social Workers?

Barry J. Nidorf

Chief Probation Officer
Los Angeles County Probation Department
Downey, California

Community corrections, in moving to adopt the sanction orientation, has placed itself squarely within the context of criminal justice rather than social work or human services or any other nonjustice context. At the same time, it has created a crisis of identity and role that has at least some practitioners in the fields of probation and parole wondering whether they should be social workers or police officers, advocates or adversaries, rehabilitators or punishers.

Important Implications

The topic discussed in this paper raises one of the most difficult issues to face community corrections in today's era of sanction orientation: determining what the modern identity and role of probation and parole officers should be. The topic is a difficult one, not only because it is complex and controversial, but because it has a number of important implications for the current and future success of probation and parole. For example: The type of answer given for a question such as "Police officer or social worker?" can have a critical effect on the credibility and standing of community corrections in the justice system and the community.

How the question is answered can also have an impact within organizations and can enhance or hinder success in carrying out their mission. The question suggests that community corrections may not have a clear idea, currently, of the nature of its identity and role.

A definition of the modern role and identity should be developed from basic principles and not derived from appearances and comparisons. Implications such as these can be nearly as important as the question they accompany; and they deserve discussion together with the question itself.

External Credibility and Standing

By adopting the sanction orientation, community corrections already is enhancing its credibility and standing in the justice system and the community. That standing can be further enhanced only by a clear determination of what role is best for the profession in the era of sanctions. There needs to be concern, however, that the role decided on will not narrow the scope of the profession's identity and activities just at a time when the sanction orientation is opening up so many opportunities for new and more effective service to the community. Most would agree that, to be fully effective and successful, probation and parole officers need to know that their professional identity and role, subject lately to many changes, continue to have validity and value. Many do know this, and they function easily and confidently within the context of sanction-oriented probation and parole, but others do not and seem troubled by the sanction orientation, thinking that it goes contrary to many long-held ideals and professional principles.

Although the sanction orientation has brought community corrections renewed recognition and has gained it increased resources, aspects of it remain difficult for some corrections workers to accept: its stress on the primacy of enforcement; its advocacy of toughness; its swift and uncompromising response to noncompliance; its ready reliance on incapacitation; and perhaps most difficult of all, its contention that the violation and incarceration of one criminal can be just as much a success as the rehabilitation of another.

Concerns of corrections workers about the sanction orientation can affect the effectiveness of their work and the work of their organizations. Such concerns need to be addressed. Community corrections' agencies need to reassure their members that their identity and role retain validity and value even as changes, which some of them find disturbing, continue to occur. This can be accomplished in two ways. First, it needs to be asserted that, despite substantial and significant changes in activities and appearances, the essential and traditional role of community corrections workers is not changed by adoption of the sanction orientation. For example, in direct response to the topic question of this paper, their role is not being changed so much that probation and parole officers are about to become police officers.

Second, we assert that the essential and traditional role of community corrections workers is compatible with the demands of the sanction orientation and is able to accommodate the broad range of activities this approach has opened for them. Unquestionably, the sanction orientation has brought many changes and new activities to community corrections. Sanction-based programs are springing up everywhere and involve probation and parole workers in activities they would not have imagined doing just a few years ago: surveillance, intrusive supervision, direct deterrence, community-based incapacitation, hand-in-glove cooperation with allied law enforcement agencies, and accelerated violation and revocation efforts. Although these activities may sometimes seem police-like in appearance, they are not so in substance. As conducted in the Los Angeles County Probation Department, they fall comfortably within what is seen as the traditional scope of probation's identity and role.

The new activities do not change probation officers' identity and role in essential ways. Certainly, they do not turn them into law enforcement officers on the beat. Some, however, may believe that just such a transformation is occurring. Some even may favor adoption of a police role for corrections workers. Community corrections must not agree with these views. As strongly as it must advocate the sanction orientation for itself, community corrections must oppose just as strongly any fundamental change that would turn its practitioners into police officers. The sanction orientation does not justify or require this. On the contrary, such action would severely reduce the range of criminal sanction options that community corrections currently commands, and it would deny the justice system the unique role community corrections plays and the perspective it provides.

Years ago, it made no sense that some people wanted to think of probation and parole officers as social workers. Today, it makes no better sense that others want to think of them as police officers. Each role, fine as it is in itself, has a far narrower scope and presents far fewer opportunities than the role that is already established and that needs to be kept.

A Clear Idea of Identity and Role

A question like "Police officer or social worker?" seems to suggest that community corrections may not be altogether clear yet about its own identity and role. This may not be a problem right now, although it could become one later on. It is probably too early in the conversion to the sanction orientation for community corrections to try to make definitive decisions about the modern role of probation and parole officers. Things are in flux, experimentation is everywhere, and healthy diversity is flourishing. Even so, under the sanction orientation, corrections workers probably are closer now to a clear idea of their role than they ever have been in the past.

The sanction orientation has made at least two things very clear that may have been a little fuzzy under the old rehabilitation orientation. The mission of community corrections is protection of the community; the task is enforcement of court orders. These two points were decided for it, but community corrections will need to decide for itself, sometime fairly soon, about other aspects of its identity and role. When the time for such decisions comes, what type of answer is community corrections likely to give to the question, "Who are we, and what do we do?"

If the past and present are any indicator of the future, the answer may not look much different from the question in the title of this paper. If that is the case, community corrections will be faced with a serious problem. It seems that community corrections has tended to define itself through comparisons with other professions. Years ago, there was a saying that tried to define a probation officer. It went something like this: What is a probation officer? A teacher without a classroom. A social worker without a benefit check. A psychologist without a degree. A cop without a beat. A lawyer without a shingle. A judge without a bench. The saying was appealing at first, but one soon realized that it did not answer the question it asked. It told what probation officers sometimes seem like, but it did not say what they really are.

The saying highlights a problem that has been in the corrections field for too long—the tendency to define its identity and role in terms of other people's work. This paper does the same thing when it asks: Are we police officers, or are we social workers? This is something community corrections will need to stop doing if it intends to define what its identity and role ought to be. If community corrections does not get down to the basics of its role—to what distinguishes it from other professions and makes it unique—it may never develop a clear idea for its practitioners of who they are and what they do.

Building on Basic Principles

When it comes time to clearly define a modern identity and role, community corrections will need to build its definition on basic principles, not superficial appearances and comparisons. The definition will need to reassure the justice system, the community, and corrections workers that community corrections has not abandoned its essential identity. It will need to tell everyone, in effect, that community corrections is still doing the best of what it always did, only doing it better. This is exactly what has happened with adoption of the sanction orientation, as an examination of basic principles will demonstrate.

There is one principle, more basic than any other, that will help community corrections define and explain its identity and role. If, right now, an effort had to be made to come up with the most basic possible definition of what community corrections does, and to put that definition into a single word, the word would be change. Change is what community corrections was trying to accomplish in the past under the old rehabilitation orientation; change is its objective now under the sanction orientation. The very existence of the corrections profession is based on the premise of change and on the idea that people can change, even some of those who commit criminal acts.

In our system of justice, convicted persons are entitled to a fair assessment of their ability to change. Some of those, judged able to change, are given the opportunity—in their normal environment—to prove that they can change. Corrections workers, as change agents, are to motivate and monitor their effort. If offenders fail to change within their own environment, their environment will be changed for them. Change, thought of in this way, has been community corrections' stock-in-trade from the beginning, and continues to be. Change has been the underlying reason for the activities of community corrections' practitioners from John Augustus right up to today. The activities may be described with big words—rehabilitation, restitution, deterrence, incapacitation—but the words all mean "change." All types of techniques can be used—counseling, observation, intrusion, or electronic gadgets that beep and buzz—but the intended result of all the techniques, old or new, is change.

In the past, community corrections sometimes got a little vague and fuzzy about the type of change that it was trying to effect. With too much confidence in its ability to change criminal behavior, and too much optimism about the ability of some criminals to change, community corrections doggedly tried to rehabilitate many who, in hindsight, had never been habilitated. Community corrections cannot afford such a mistake again.

Now, with the kinds of habitual and violent criminals it is called on to supervise, it must equip itself with a precise definition of the type of change it seeks to effect. The change that community corrections has always tried to effect is removal of the individual's criminal activity from the community. There are two ways the criminal's activity can be removed from the community. The first is for a criminal, while remaining in the community, to give up crime and live a law-abiding life. In this rehabilitation scenario, the criminal is changed; his or her environment is not. The second way is for a criminal, unable or unwilling to give up crime, to be effectively incapacitated—in the community perhaps but more likely in jail or prison. In this recidivism scenario, the criminal is not changed; his or her environment is.

Generally speaking, community corrections has been comfortable with the first scenario, trying hard to change the criminal without having to change his or her environment. It has been less comfortable with the second scenario, considering the need to change the criminal's environment as being in some sense a failure to achieve the primary objective of rehabilitation. Some corrections workers seem to still feel this way. So, there are concerns that adoption of the sanction orientation means discarding traditional principles and losing validity and value for the community corrections role. So too, there is difficulty understanding how corrections can assert that now it is equally successful if it incarcerates one criminal while it rehabilitates another.

Clearly, though, if it is understood that the correctional change effort always has been, and continues to be, removal of criminal activity from the community, it also will be understood that rehabilitation and incapacitation are essentially similar and equally valid methods of effecting that change. They are, simply, the two sides of a single coin. There is a point, however, at which the sanction orientation differs from the rehabilitation orientation and requires a major adjustment in the thinking and approach of community corrections. That point is the shifting of the primary focus of our change effort from the criminal to the community.

Accomplishment of corrections' change effort through a criminal's giving up crime—the rehabilitation scenario—remains the most desirable approach to removing criminal activity from the community. But if a criminal cannot or will not change within the environment of the community, then the sanction orientation requires that community corrections must, for the sake of community protection, immediately and without compunction, act to change the environment in which the criminal functions. If some corrections workers have a need to hold on to the term rehabilitation as a description of what they do, they can think of the primary, change-based task of community corrections as that of "rehabilitating" the community. In a broad sense, this is a legitimate characterization of what the sanction orientation does when it makes the community, not the criminal, the direct and primary object of the change effort that community corrections has traditionally called "rehabilitation." The change effort itself, even though different in focus and object under the sanction orientation, remains essentially what it has always been.

Conclusion

The topic of this paper has served to bring discussion to exactly where it needs to be in a continuing review of the conversion of community corrections to the sanction orientation. The issue presented is complex and controversial and probably has many more implications for the current and future success of community corrections than just those that are touched on here. The topic is critically important and deserves a great deal more thought and discussion. It will be no easy task for community corrections to decide on a modern identity and role for itself that will be consistent with its basic principles and essential traditions; retain the full scope and range of its accustomed activities and influence; define community corrections workers by what they are rather than how they seem in comparison with others; and, perhaps most important of all, assure all corrections practitioners of the continued validity and value of the profession to which they belong.

One step in defining identity and role will always be to determine what should not be included. In that regard, and in response to the question that is the title of this paper, the answer regarding probation and parole officers should be this: We are neither police officers nor social workers. Rather, we are community correctional workers with our own identity and role. For if we are police officers, why not arm all of us, put us in "black and whites" and let us arrest all who break the law? But then, if we were police officers, why would we be needed? Why not just turn our responsibilities over to the larger and better financed police departments, as some have already suggested. As for being social workers, probation and parole officers should say: We are neither trained nor equipped to do that job. Even if we were, as social workers we would lack the ability to protect the community effectively, and we would lack the coercive sanction options needed to enforce court orders.

Probation and parole officers should say: We are community correctional workers who strive to protect the community by changing the criminal or his or her environment in an effort to remove criminal activity from the community.

Putting "Community" into Community Corrections

Donald G. Evans

President
Donald G. Evans & Associates
Toronto, Ontario, Canada

We are facing a crisis in criminal justice today that in many ways is related to a shift in the way society is being policed. This shift is a move from a reliance on informal mechanisms of social control to more formal mechanisms backed by the state's power to punish. However, we are becoming increasingly aware that the scale of imprisonment in our society is outstretching our ability to pay.

In the past, we relied on the exercise of informal social control in the home, school, and workplace. Formal policing occurred only in the streets and in public places. Today, there is a marked change in social control strategies, and the police now often must intervene in the home because of family violence, in the schools because of violence and drugs, and in the workplace because of violence and sexual assault.

Formal mechanisms of social control now reach deep into areas where formerly there was informal social control. This breakdown adds to the burdens already being placed on government as it tries to protect public safety. Governments have responded to this environment with legislation and harsher punishments, which in the process has created a sense of futility and public alienation. However, we are losing the fight against crime. We have boxed ourselves into a "prison" that disempowers us. Slowly, society is realizing that government has a limited capacity to punish.

The criminal justice system is a response to a problem—not the solution. Crime is a crisis that tells us something is terribly wrong. We have to ask ourselves: What are we learning from this crisis? What are we learning about our communities? What are we learning about our institutions? What are we learning about ourselves?

We need to realize that "policing" means more than just letting the local police force walk its beat, and "corrections" means more than just incarcerating offenders. We need to work together to emphasize policies and programs that will strengthen the informal mechanisms of social control and build community.

Community Involvement

We have spent the last decade and a half putting "corrections" into community corrections. We have tougher community programs, and the programs have become more like prison. Still, the promise of crime reduction eludes us. Community corrections has come to rely on punitive social control and has ignored the larger issue of building and strengthening other mechanisms of social control.

In criminal justice, as in other areas, governments rarely offer choices to citizens and rarely use the community to resolve problems. We need to seek ways to meaningfully and substantially include the community.

The American Probation and Parole Association has embarked on a major effort to get probation and parole agencies to work toward community justice. Community justice can become the means to revive a sense of community and social solidarity. It involves finding ways to reduce neighborhood fragmentation and resolve intergenerational and multicultural tensions in our communities. It means working to respect human dignity and self-worth and doing this by reducing unemployment and poverty. This concept stresses the principles of fairness, equity, and appropriate community-based sanctions for criminal behavior. It envisions a range of responses to offending behavior in a community rather than an institutional setting. Community justice will involve alternative delivery systems for social and criminal justice services that include private-public partnerships, local citizen boards, and volunteers. It will take community involvement, cooperation, and collaboration between diverse areas, such as social services, education, industry, and the criminal justice system, to restore a sense of security and well-being to our society. This is not a matter of just "correcting." It is a matter of justice and fairness.

To accomplish this, we need to put the community back into community corrections. However, first, we need to overcome some obstacles to the community's involvement, which include the following:

1. The community usually does not realize the importance of the service provided by probation and parole agencies. While probation and parole provides direct services to convicted offenders, their services indirectly affect everyone in the community.

2. The public has a negative perception of the nature of the service. Probation and parole agencies serve people who often have uncomfortable problems—such as substance abuse, illiteracy, and sexual deviance—that accompany their criminal offenses.

3. Public relations' efforts often are reactive rather than proactive. Information on probation and parole services generally is relayed to the public only when an offender "fails" or commits a serious offense. Managing these events puts the agency into a defensive role and makes it more difficult to communicate the worthwhile services the agency offers the community.

To counteract these obstacles to community involvement, a number of very creative and innovative programs have been initiated by a number of probation and parole agencies. In Madison, Wisconsin, the probation department has adopted the principle of community policing and developed a neighborhood probation program. This program is a back-to-basics, low cost, high visibility effort to bring corrections to the community.

In Vermont, they restructured their approach to adult probation and developed a statewide system of probation that aimed at having the sentences of 60 percent of the cases determined by local reparative community boards comprised of citizens, including a victim representative. After conviction, nonviolent offenders are referred by the judge to the local board. The offender is required to appear, and the offense is reviewed and an appropriate sentence determined, usually involving restitution, community service, or victim-offender mediation. In this approach, local communities are more directly involved in the sentencing and reintegration efforts.

In New Zealand and Australia, there is growing interest in using a method of restorative justice that is referred to as Family Group Conferencing or, sometimes, Group Conferencing. This approach involves the offenders (who have admitted guilt) taking part in a conference that includes their family and friends, the victims, and their family and friends. The conference is facilitated by a trained local official, such as a police officer, teacher, or probation officer. During the conference, the participants discuss the offense, its impact on everyone involved, and a plan for the offender to repair the harm done.

These examples work because they involve the community in correctional programming and enhance the community's self-determination rather than make the community a passive "victim" or spectator to the problems offending behavior causes.

Challenges

Probation and parole agencies face three challenges to launching a community involvement effort—lack of time, limited resources, and lack of expertise. Time and resource constraints will continue to be an issue for probation and parole. The offender population is increasing without corresponding budget increases. Caseloads are at an all-time high, putting a strain on resources. This has put probation and parole officers in a reactive posture. They spend the majority of their time responding to crisis situations and have little time for public relations efforts. It is ironic that the major inhibitors to community involvement are the very things that make it a necessity.

Probation and parole agencies have tended to be concerned about their organizational capacity to meet the problems of lack of time and limited resources. By looking for solutions to these problems only in their own organizations, they miss the opportunity to think and act outside of their organizational box. If they conceive of the problem as one of operational rather than organizational capacity, that is, capacity beyond staffing and budgets allocated to them, new possibilities are realized. Partnerships become possible, and new alliances with other social, criminal justice, and community agencies come into existence, creating a sum greater than its individual parts.

A lack of expertise is more a matter of perception than reality. Many of the skills sought when hiring probation and parole staff—communication skills, organizational skills, and problem-solving skills—are the very skills needed for community involvement initiatives. These requirements may require some role change on the part of probation and parole staff. For some, it may mean a move away from direct service providers to problem solvers, network managers, community developers, and educators. Furthermore, probation and parole staff may have access to various community groups, such as membership organizations, churches, service clubs, and alumni groups, where they have opportunities to educate the community about their agency's programs and rally community support. Officers and supervisors simply need to be given administrative support for making community involvement a priority.

We need to make community corrections a reality. No formal mechanism of social control is as potent as the informal control provided by cohesive communities. Crime is an emotion-ridden issue. We must capture these emotions and transform the public's fear and apprehension into an energetic and proactive community response. Intermediate sanctions—or any other sanctioning concept—cannot work in a vacuum. We need strong communities and cooperation among all organizations and agencies that address the social problems of our communities. We cannot provide public safety alone, but together we can become more secure and less fearful of one another.

References

Braithwaite, John. 1995. Reintegrative Sharing, Republicanism, and Policy. In H. D. Barlow. *Crime and Public Policy: Putting Theory to Work.* Boulder, CO: Westview Press, Inc.

Evans, Donald G. 1992. Innovative Neighborhood Project Uses Community Policing Principles. *Corrections Today.* August.

Fulton, Betsy. 1996. Restoring Hope Through Community Partnerships, the Real Deal in Crime Control. American Probation and Parole Association.

Repinsky, Harold E. 1989. Issues of Citizen Involvement in Policing. *Crime and Delinquency.* July.

Reeves, Rhonda. 1992. Perspective: Community Justice. *State Government News.* November, 35:11 pp. 35-36.

Community Service: A Partnership That Works

Richard J. Maher

Supervising United States Probation Officer
United States District Court
Northern District of Georgia Probation Office
Atlanta, Georgia

In spite of a massive building program costing two billion dollars over the past five years, the Federal Bureau of Prisons still operates a system 25 percent overcapacity. Even with current expansion plans, the situation will worsen by the end of the decade.

This is not to say that, in the interest of public safety, many of our prisoners are not treated as they should be. In fact, it is appalling that many of our most dangerous offenders revolve in and out of the prison door. Crime is a terrible and serious threat that must be addressed. Thefts and acts of violence that touch our lives and our loved ones are frightening. Rates of recidivism are as high as ever, and the public seems frustrated and frightened.

Nonetheless, exaggerated fear results in calling for all offenders to be placed behind bars; this is exploited by ill-advised politicians droning the tired adage, "if you do the crime, you do the time." Punishments are often disproportionate to the crimes and result in undue social and financial cost. Most unfortunate is that at least one-third of those sent to prisons are not only redeemable, but can be valuable assets to their communities. Contrary to our goal of protecting the community by preventing an offender's return to crime, we sometimes perpetuate policies that place us all at risk. It is time that we in probation assert our expertise. We must take the initiative to educate ourselves, the public, and our political leadership about what works and what does not.

Guidelines

Beginning in 1984, federal legislation mandated a series of punitive initiatives, including federal guideline sentencing, in part designed to eliminate real or perceived sentencing disparity. Additional laws passed in 1986 and 1987 set mandatory sentences for drug offenders. These measures have crippled formerly effective community-based supervision programs in federal court districts and have drawn a great deal of criticism for their lack of consideration for intermediate sanctions. Sentencing guidelines often unnecessarily force incarceration of nonviolent, first-time offenders. Though unintentional, the current guidelines disproportionally and irrationally penalize African-Americans. Indeed, critics charge that aside from being both costly and complicated, guidelines often are devoid of compassion and common sense. In fact, guidelines represent a total rejection of rehabilitative concerns.

Proponents of sentencing guidelines feel that with adjustments, guidelines can be fair and will accommodate an array of alternative sentences. A now abandoned United States Sentencing Commission study promised to broaden the use of community service and other intermediate sanctions. Those who administer local programs were hopeful that guidelines would offer a range of options for nonviolent offenders and that resources to screen, place, and supervise offenders would be given administrative and material support. However, given the current political climate, reform efforts have been abandoned. Clearly, court-ordered community service programs operating in several federal court districts have worked for the court, and more important, they have worked for the community. In districts where offenders' skills and talents have been used to benefit the community, the response has been one of appreciation often shown through citizen support and recognition.

A Successful Program

The Northern District of Georgia Probation Office has operated a successful program for more than a decade. Between 1985 and 1996, offenders have contributed over 300,000 hours in community service work while completing many sophisticated projects valued in excess of $3 million. The program has received positive recognition in the media and has been given numerous awards from civic, governmental, and nonprofit groups throughout the district. The success in the Northern District of Georgia has now been duplicated in several other federal court districts including the districts of Nebraska, Eastern Tennessee, and South Carolina. These programs have provided an alternative to incarceration in which everyone wins. The system and the community have realized that offenders, when properly directed, are a positive asset.

Effective community service programs provide an opportunity for offenders to make amends with dignity. Instead of being their wardens and jailers, corrections workers become their teachers and coaches. Through these efforts, offenders are encouraged and helped, and personal and public attitudes are changed. Rick Flinn, director of Atlanta's Fox Theater, described to the *Atlanta Journal* his experience with federal court-ordered workers. "At first, there was a certain amount of distaste involved, but that was more than counteracted by the work that has been done." Flinn oversaw, among others, an accountant, a carpet and drapery cleaner, and a sculptor who remodeled plasterwork. "If they were all in jail," he said, "we would be paying thousands of dollars for these services. It is more effective in rehabilitating them than if they were sitting around with other criminals." Some offenders placed at the Fox Theater were later offered employment there or received help finding work elsewhere.

An Environmental Improvement Effort

One Northern District of Georgia project involved cooperation between the probation office, the Georgia Mental Health Institute, the Fernbank Museum of Natural History, and an area neighborhood organization. The museum, a $44 million project, opened in the summer of 1992. The museum's main building is a four-story, 150,000-square-foot structure with two stories underground. It is located on a twenty-five-acre property. Existing houses on the property also were renovated with assistance from community service workers and are currently being used as offices and classrooms. The excavation and demolition required for the project was extensive, and much of the debris from the Fernbank site was destined to consume valuable landfill space.

However, at the time excavation and demolition began, community service workers at the Georgia Mental Health Institute (GMHI) were beginning work cleaning out a drained lake bed, which had been abandoned in previous years and had become a swamp engulfed in kudzu. The five-acre gully bred mosquitos and rats and was a nuisance to the hospital and surrounding neighborhood. The court community service coordinator was involved with both projects. Taking the initiative, he was able to assemble a group including the Fernbank contractor, the mental hospital maintenance department, and individuals from the neighborhood adjacent to the hospital. Together, they accomplished an ambitious environmental improvement project in which fill dirt from the museum site was used for the hospital's lake bed project.

Much of the project's organizational task was delegated to court-ordered community service workers. Their work expanded to include grounds projects over the hospital's entire thirty-five acres. When the project was finished, more than 2,000 tandem truck loads of dirt had been placed in the lake bed. The contractor involved saved an estimated $35,000 in dumping fees; Fernbank saved $100,000 in project development costs; and the Georgia Mental Health Institute received more than $100,000 worth of fill dirt. Perhaps most important, offenders' self-esteem was raised by pride in their service to Fernbank, the Georgia Mental Health Institute, and the local community.

One offender involved with this project was hired full-time by the Fernbank museum. A former marijuana grower, he describes his opportunity as a dream come true. Since being hired to work with the museum, his previous experience as a stone mason, grant writer, and his knowledge of pre-Columbian artifacts has been valuable. Through his effort and opportunity, both he and the community have been optimally served. He has completed his sentence, continued his employment and, given his devotion to family and community, he is a model citizen by any standard.

This offender's accomplishment is only one of many similar stories of the Atlanta program. Over the years, many court-ordered community service workers secure employment at their assigned agencies or as a result of contacts made at the agency. Examples include a former food service worker who was trained and employed as a nurse's aide at the Georgia Mental Health Institute. Another was a disabled plumber who could no longer pursue his trade, but was hired as a bus driver after completing 600 hours for the Atlanta Senior Citizen Services. Still another offender obtained a sales job earning $40,000 annually, as compared with his previous job as a construction supervisor earning $18,000. In each case, through becoming familiar with the offender, the community opened its doors rather than rejecting and punishing. The result is that we all enjoy a safer and enriched community.

Though only a small fraction of those convicted have been given the opportunity to participate in the Atlanta community service program, and only one probation officer's duties are dedicated to placement and project coordination, the accomplishments are notable.

Notable Programs and Placements

The program involves men and women convicted of nonviolent federal crimes, most of whom have no prior record. Some notable placements include the following:

1. A chef at an upscale Atlanta restaurant, convicted on drug charges, cooked for the Cerebral Palsy Center.
2. A builder in Norcross, convicted of income tax evasion, worked as a construction coordinator for Gwinnett County Habitat for Humanity, performing 530 hours more than the 1,920 required.
3. Community service workers have been placed over the past several years at elementary schools as teachers' aides, tutors and clerks.
4. A former athlete worked with Special Olympics, earning a Volunteer of the Year award.
5. Doctors convicted of student loan fraud and dentists convicted of tax evasion worked in community clinics.
6. A psychiatrist worked in a county jail helping treat inmates.

7. An artist restored a severely water-damaged antique painting at the DeKalb Addiction Clinic.
8. A heavy equipment operator, convicted of having used his equipment to clear runways for drug traffickers, used his talent and equipment for a variety of landscape and environmental projects.

Some notable projects include the following:

1. Restorations on circa-1895 greenhouses at the former Asa G. Candler, Jr., mansion, now home to the DeKalb Addiction Clinic.
2. Concrete poured for an elevator shaft at Glen Castle, a housing shelter for homeless families.
3. Dormitory facilities for The Atlanta Task Force for the Homeless were built at offender expense with community service labor.
4. Construction of Phoenix House, a development of Project Interconnections. This was the state's first comprehensive residential facility for the homeless mentally ill.
5. Staff assistance provided to Jerusalem House for homeless AIDS patients.
6. A play about drug abuse performed by a group of offenders and non-offenders. The play received $65,000 in funding from foundations and business groups. It was performed at the Academy Theater, at area schools, and in state prisons.
7. Between 1991 and 1996, five annual projects completed for the United States Forestry Service involving 220 offenders. They have completed about 8,800 hours of work in the Chattahoochee National Forest which include building camp sites, a helicopter hanger, and bridges, and participating in trail restoration and wildlife preservation efforts.
9. Staffing of the Georgia Lions Light House mobile eye clinic by federal community service workers in 1995 and 1996. This service performs glaucoma screening and provides eye glass prescriptions for the financially disadvantaged.

Hopefully, increasing success with community service and other intermediate sanctions will replace the notion that only prison constitutes true retribution. With proper screening and follow up, the Northern District of Georgia's experience has demonstrated that as much as forty hours of community service per week performed for a full year can successfully substitute for incarceration. Often, these sentences can be combined with confinement in a halfway house, Sanction Center, or include electronic monitoring. Among other benefits, such sentences keep families together and deliver valuable services to the communty.

Atlanta is not unique. Communities' needs and offenders' abilities are much the same throughout the country. We need only to develop confidence among the public and the political leadership to show that we have a rational system that works. We are not alone; business, civic leaders, and others will be supportive. Still, criminal justice professionals must take the initiative or this valuable resource will continue to be ignored at untold and unnecessary cost.

10

The Salvation Army Formula: Soup, Soap, and Salvation

M. Patrick McCabe

Director of Correctional Services
The Salvation Army
Sarasota, Florida

Introduction

This paper addresses the correctional services' role of the Salvation Army in the United States. Specific attention is given to the means used to successfully deal with hundreds of thousands of criminal offenders.

The founder of the Salvation Army, William Booth, stated, "Go for souls and go for the worst," and the Salvation Army has always worked with even the most violent offenders. Through its bible study classes, prison visitation, and Christmas toy program, it has sought out and counseled persons others have classified as hopeless.

There are, however, certain limitations when it comes to community services. The Salvation Army does not specialize in mental health, and it is ill equipped to deal with psychotics who pose a serious threat to public safety. Nor does it advocate community programs for those predators who must be removed for the good of the public. Furthermore, the Army does not become involved in lockdown programs where legal restraints require close security.

With all others, however, a basic Army formula has evolved known as the three S's: Soup, Soap, and Salvation. It is time-tested and is the force behind the Army's movement. As simple as this formula may be, it may be the solution to the chaos that currently plagues our criminal justice system. If applied properly, the formula can be an integral part of all criminal justice correctional efforts.

History

In England in 1865, William Booth emerged from the chaos of industrial society and offered hope for humanity. English philosophers of that day such as Jeremy Bentham and Herbert Spencer spoke of pleasure and pain and individual choice. Punishments were severe and applied uniformly with no accounting for age, circumstances, or mental capacity. William Booth, on the other hand, was concerned with the salvation of the soul and redemption of human lives.

Despite the harsh nature of the punishments, criminal justice problems were similar to those today. Prisons were overcrowded, crime was rampant, and violence was not uncommon. In later years, this led William Booth to remark:

> I might have chosen to devote my life to the interest of the criminal world. The hundreds of thousands of poor wretches who are pining in the criminal cells while we are sitting here at ease ought to have our sympathy and help. We havedone something for the criminal, but it is only the commencement of a mighty work the Army is to do for this unhappy class.

The Army's early efforts were significant. With others, they were able to initiate reforms at Newgate Prison and the workhouses. They formed the Prison Gate Brigade and established the first halfway house. They assisted thousands of offenders, ex-offenders, and their families through the social services movement.

The earliest recorded Salvation Army corrections efforts in America occurred in New York City in 1880. George Scott Railton and the "Seven Hallelujah Lassies" had come to the United States that year. His earliest efforts were staged at Harry Hill's Variety House, which was a saloon and music hall. There were over forty English-speaking theaters and a multitude of music and variety houses in New York City. Everyone who could afford a ticket went for the entertainment. Harry Hill allowed the Army to take the stage on Sundays. He saw it more as a performance and offered to pay, but Railton refused the income.

The first meeting was a disappointment, but soon the Army was ensconced in the Hudson River Hall and had secured their first convert, Ash Barrel Jimmy, a drunken homeless person. Jimmy had received his name when a policeman hauled him to the station still frozen to the ash barrel that he called home. The judge ordered him to attend the Salvation Army act at the variety hall. Jimmy was converted that night and became one of the Army's spokesmen.

The corrections movement in the United States moved quickly. The earliest jail services began in Hartford, Connecticut, and Sacramento, California, in 1885. In 1887, the Prison Gate Brigade emerged and was responsible for housing and finding employment for persons released from jails and prisons in several major cities. The first prison ministry began at San Quentin in 1894. A hostel for discharged prisoners was opened in San Ramon, California, in 1897. The "Lifers Club" was initiated by an ex-offender at the Massachusetts State Penitentiary in 1904. Shortly after that, prison visitation became a part of every corps. In 1887, a full-fledged Salvation Army Corps was formed at San Quentin with thirty soldiers. Over the next twenty-five years, corps were formed at Michigan State Prison, the Indiana State Boys' Reformatory, the Oklahoma State Prison, Folsom Prison, and state prisons in New Jersey and Kansas.

During the 1920s, parole programs were developed in New York, California, and Massachusetts. Nearly half of the parolees involved had been convicted of violent crimes. Also in 1920, the Army started its federal involvement through chaplain appointments at Atlanta and McNeil Island. Through the ensuing decades and up to the present, the Salvation Army has been a willing and active partner in community-based programs that few others were willing or able to embrace. The Salvation Army, with its history and philosophy of caring for those with whom no one else was either willing or able to work, is a ready partner for the county, state, and federal community corrections efforts. Today, thousands of prisoners are being channeled through the Salvation Army's contract and general residential program in virtually every state in the nation. These programs are extremely effective.

Soup, Soap, and Salvation

The range of programs provided by the Salvation Army begins with prenatal care and continues through senior-citizen activities. In between, they involve youth, juveniles, the homeless, the addicted, and victims of disaster. At each level, the purpose is the same—reclamation of the individual. Much of what is done is preventive and successfully diverts thousands of persons from the criminal justice system. Others work with the offenders in an effort to rebuild their world. In all instances, the formula is Soup, Soap, and Salvation.

Soup: Nutrition and good health are key factors in diverting persons from crime. It is impossible to rebuild a person's life while he or she is hungry or sick. The first step is to make the person physically fit.

In 1994, the Salvation Army served over 18 million meals in the United States. Over 1.5 million persons were provided medical and pharmaceutical assistance. Clinics and hospitals served over 200,000. Emergency disaster service was provided to 3.2 million individuals. Most of this consisted of food and medical items. The Salvation Army is unsurpassed in the service of providing "soup."

Soap: The Salvation Army also recognizes that a person cannot build a successful life without an image of self-worth and a strong sense of dignity. You must clean persons up, give them a decent place to stay, and offer them the opportunity to derive satisfaction from honest labor. In 1994, casework services were provided to 11 million persons in the United States. Thirty-nine thousand persons were referred to jobs. Nearly five million persons were provided extended and temporary lodging.

The Army also is very active in youth programs that stress hygiene and virtue training. In 1994, day care was provided for 32,000 children. Children's residential programs served 20,000 persons. Community centers and Boys and Girls Clubs had 103,000 members. The Army has demonstrated competence in fulfilling the "soap" portion of its three S's.

Salvation: William Booth's theology is posited on two basic premises. The first is conversion—accepting the fact that individuals can only escape from the consequences of original sin through the grace of Christ. The second is that after conversion the sinful tendencies remain but through a love for God, a belief in themselves, and a love for humanity, their sinful tendencies can be overcome.

Thus, the basic premise of the Salvation Army is spiritual. This is the principle that has guided it to its greatest success over the past 131 years. Care and spiritual commitment have changed the lives of the majority of people the Salvation Army has dealt with from its earliest beginnings to modern times.

There is, however, a humanitarian side marked by the Army creed, "Heart to God. Hand to Man." This philosophy has resulted in the Army's becoming the world's largest social service agency. It is from this philosophy that our correctional programs have emerged.

Whether it is a reclamation of faith or a basic commitment to human values, the end result is the critical factor. In the correctional field, one or the other or both must be accomplished if the person is to be diverted from the criminal justice system. It is because of the way in which this is accomplished that the Army has such high levels of success, and it is because of this success that the criminal justice field relies so heavily on the Salvation Army's services.

Again, the premise is simple—the Army believes in the absolute worth of every human being. No person, regardless of past behavior, is beyond redemption. All programs are designed to bring the positive features of the human spirit forward and provide each person with the opportunity to lead a proud and productive life.

The Army's spiritual programs in correctional facilities are widespread. Some form of corrections services occurs in each of the ninety-eight countries they serve. In 1994, 442,000 prisoners were visited worldwide. There were 283,000 visits in the United States. Also in the United States there were 6,000 bible study correspondents who submitted over 106,000 lessons. More than 13,000 offenders committed themselves to God. The Christmas Toy Lift Program allowed several thousand inmates the opportunity to select and send toys to their children. The Salvation Army is a silent partner in this program.

The community corrections programs are even more extensive. Worldwide in 1993, 305,000 police court cases were assisted. A total of 38,000 people were helped on discharge from jail or prison. In the United States in 1994, 18,000 persons were assigned to the supervision of the Salvation Army. Some 26,000 ex-offenders or their families received assistance. In all, 250 communities in the United States were affected by these services.

Residential programs are varied and plentiful. Qualified ex-offenders are eligible for services from the 118 Salvation Army Rehabilitation Centers. These are residential centers that assist in transitional housing and offer other social services. Seventeen Harbor Light Centers are also available for intensive drug and alcohol treatment. A network of 4,319 Salvation Army centers and service units provide emergency services and temporary housing for released prisoners and their families.

The largest Salvation Army contact facility is the Army Correctional Community Center in Chicago, Illinois. A part of the larger Freedom Center complex, the center houses up to 175 federal inmates. This center was opened in 1975 and received American Correctional Association accreditation in 1980. Special services include: a resident advisor, transitional counseling, employment services, drug aftercare, family reconciliation, life skills classes, and a full range of recreational activities. Instruction in reading, writing, and general equivalency diploma preparation is also available. Developing basic job skills in typing and other office work is included in the training curriculum. Chaplaincy is available at the offender's request. A similar program is offered in Milwaukee where forty state inmates are afforded shelter and extensive, structured programs.

In Florida, four Army centers offer housing and programs for over 125 federal, state, and county offenders. Each of these centers is designed to provide personal growth and decision-making skills. The goal is to prepare individuals to make a positive contribution to their community.

During 1995, the Salvation Army assisted in more than 125,000 court cases. These programs include probation of misdemeanors, pretrial intervention, supervised release on recognizance, intensive probation, and several others.

Nearly 57,000 cases were assigned to the Salvation Army's misdemeanor probation program in Florida. Through special statutory authorization, the Salvation Army supervises this probation program in twenty-four Florida counties. Each program is funded through monthly $40 payments made by probationers to cover the cost of supervision. Fees are waived when there is a demonstrated inability to pay. If a probationer is capable of paying, but refuses to, violations of probation are filed. There is no cost to the counties that are served by this program. During 1995, the Salvation Army supervised over one million community service hours and collected over $5 million in fines and restitution for these counties.

Many programs, such as the Life Management Program in Florida's Sarasota, Volusia, and Pinellas counties, use volunteers and professionals to conduct life-skills and counseling services. This is based on the belief that probationers serving terms for misdemeanors can benefit from personal attention.

The program was designed for probationers lacking the ability to cope in today's stressful environment.

The Life Management Program is a true partnership effort. Early planning sessions involving court and county officials were crucial. Many of these officials were recruited early and became an integral part of the planning cycle. Life-skills classes are offered in behavior modification, anger control, employment readiness, money management, and substance abuse; a class for repeat offenders is offered, as well. Some are free and are taught by volunteers, while others require a nominal fee. In Sarasota, a local foundation supplies scholarship grants that provide funds for those unable to pay. In 1995, 1,500 persons were enrolled in Sarasota County.

For offenders with more intense social problems, a one-on-one program is available. Volunteers are matched with probationers, and they meet for an hour each week to discuss the probation court requirements and their personal situations. The volunteers come from all walks of life and are selected for their ability to listen and serve as role models. These volunteers can have a significant positive impact on the life of the probationer. When contact is made and trust develops, the volunteers are a valuable asset in putting the probationer's life on the right track. In 1993, 159 persons participated in this program in Sarasota County.

Other referral programs that fall under this life-management umbrella include: classes in general equivalency diploma preparation, parenting skills, and English as a second language. Counseling also is provided on AIDS and mental health issues, and small business consulting is available. Once assigned, the probationers are involved for the duration of their probation period.

Salvation comes in many forms, and the Salvation Army leads the way in reclaiming the lives of their correctional clients.

Conclusion

This paper has presented a simple formula that the Salvation Army has successfully applied for the past 131 years. Soup, Soap, and Salvation are critical elements of the Army's efforts. However, the three S's are more than just concepts. They constitute a spiritual and humanitarian approach that presumes all persons are equal in their ability to regain their dignity and lead productive lives. The key is that the Army encourages the human factor—the heart-to-heart approach.

Another major Army principle is "Feed the Corps." This refers to the Army's desire to bring its clients into the church and make them members of the spiritual and social service team. Just like "Ash Barrel Jimmy," these persons often become leaders in helping others in the same predicament.

Our communities could learn from this example. Treatment programs, no matter how effective, will have little lasting effect if the offenders are not afforded the opportunity to rejoin the honest world. Too often, barriers are erected which make it difficult for these "converts" to lead a normal life.

It is important for us to afford these people the opportunity to earn their place in the mainstream of society. Then, through their example, the thousands of "Ash Barrel Jimmy's" on our streets and in our prisons can also be "converted" to free, hard-working citizens. An unidentified inmate summarized the positive effect of the Salvation Army:

> It is the human touch in this world that counts. The touch of your hand in mine. Which means far more to the faint of heart than shelter and food and wine. For shelter is gone when the day is over and bread lasts only a day. But the touch of a hand and the sound of a voice sing on in the soul always.

11

Day Reporting Centers

Elizabeth L. Curtin

Deputy Director
Crime and Justice Foundation
Boston, Massachusetts

History

Day centers were first established in England by the probation service in 1974. These "Day Attendance Centres" were "aimed at diverting from custody the older, petty, persistent offenders whose offending seemed to stem from social inadequacy, and subjecting them to a course of intensive, structured training" (Mair 1988).

After visiting with the creators, staff, and clients of the British centers, the Crime and Justice Foundation introduced an adapted version to criminal justice experts in the United States. In 1986, the Foundation worked with the Hampden County Sheriff's Department in Springfield, Massachusetts to establish the first American day reporting center. The following year, the Crime and Justice Foundation began operation of the Metropolitan Day Reporting Center (MDRC) in Boston, Massachusetts. Both of these centers were originally designed as early release options for sentenced inmates incarcerated in county correctional facilities.

Today, there are over 115 day reporting centers in at least twenty-two states. According to a recent publication on day reporting centers by the National Institute of Justice (NIJ 1995), some of these centers are operated by private agencies, but most of the newer ones are operated by public agencies. While the original programs targeted an already incarcerated population, many of the newer centers are designed for use with a variety of offenders including those sentenced directly to the centers, pretrial detainees, probationers, and parolees, and for juveniles as well as adult offenders.

Definition

What is a day reporting center? First, it is a concept rather than a "model." As a concept, it can be adapted to the particular needs and goals of a variety of situations with a variety of populations. There is an unfortunate tendency to try to duplicate a "model" program that works well in another area, only to realize that it just is not effective at home. Each individual jurisdiction has its own goals, needs, resources, politics, and individuals which make it unique and which requires programs that are in sync with those variables.

The National Institute of Justice (1995) defines a day reporting center as "an intermediate sanction that blends high levels of control with intensive delivery of services needed by offenders." This blend includes supervision, sanctions, and services coordinated from the center itself. Day reporting centers are intended to provide a structured transition for offenders from being in conflict with the law to being contributing members of the community.

Supervision activities are intended to address public safety concerns and provide structure for the offenders' activities. These include preparing a daily itinerary of activities, frequently contacting the center (in person, by telephone, or via electronic monitoring), submitting to frequent and random drug testing, as well as random community checks. Program sanctions stress accountability and restitution to the community through curfews, monitoring of court-ordered payments, and mandatory activities such as community work service.

Addressing service needs provides the offender with the support and means to deal with the often complex issues surrounding substance abuse, mental health education, vocational training, and job placement assistance. The center serves as the locus for all activities. Some activities may be delivered at the center, while others may be provided out in the community. This use of community resources avoids duplication of services and allows offenders to be connected to resources that will continue after their legal obligations with the center are met.

Day reporting centers appear to be cost-effective correctional options. Average operating costs are less than incarceration but more than some other community corrections programs. The National Institute of Justice (NIJ 1995) compared cost information on thirty-three day reporting centers and found the average daily cost per offender to be $35.04. The study also found a wide range of average daily costs from $10 a day to over $100 a day; public programs were found to be less expensive to operate than private programs; and the operating costs go up with more program options and stricter monitoring procedures.

Description of Operation

The Crime and Justice Foundation has operated the Metropolitan Day Reporting Center (MDRC) in Boston since 1987. Referrals to the center come from a variety of sources: classification boards, case workers, probation officers, district attorneys, judges, police, and others. The population served includes sentenced and pretrial detainees from Suffolk County Sheriff's Department and probationers from Suffolk County courts. Suffolk County is a major urban area that includes the city of Boston. The daily count at the Metropolitan Day Reporting Center has been averaging around thirty, and has been as high as seventy-five. To date, more than 1,550 offenders have been admitted to the program, and close to 70 percent have successfully met the terms of their contracts.

The criteria which guide eligibility and admission to the program include that potential participants:

- be charged with or convicted of a property offense, drug- or alcohol-related offense, or minor person offense
- be within 120 days of release if sentenced, have been held for forty-eight hours if pretrial, or indicate high risk and high need, if probationer
- have a verifiable residence and legal means of support
- agree to abide by the conditions of the contract

Case managers work with each client to develop an individualized client contract intended to address specific needs and to outline supervision requirements. To fulfill their contracts, clients must:

- check in to the center in person according to an approved schedule
- submit an itinerary that includes locations, names, and telephone numbers for all activities
- call in to the center at scheduled times
- be available for random calls or visits at home or other locations on itinerary
- participate in all activities as planned and as stipulated in the contract
- submit to frequent and random drug testing
- comply with a set curfew
- refrain from criminal activity

Common Uses

The growth of day reporting centers has been rapid and widespread . Some states have or are developing whole networks of centers. North Carolina, for example, is currently implementing over fifty day reporting centers. To meet the needs of their new structured sentencing laws which include an intermediate sentence.

The target populations of day reporting centers are very broad based, ranging from front end (probation violators) to the back end (prerelease eligible inmates) of criminal justice systems. This variety of target populations is possible only if centers are initially developed as a concept reflecting the particular needs of the local offenders, the local criminal justice system, and the local community. Whatever the target population, day reporting centers can provide a viable option on the continuum of intermediate sanctions.

The Crime and Justice Foundation's day reporting center in Boston has received many requests for information and many visitors over the years, all interested in developing similar programs. The array of agencies represented by this group is an indication of the breadth of interest in this type of community correctional programming: judiciary, probation departments, corrections departments, private nonprofits, sheriffs, police departments, elected officials, halfway houses, and universities.

Day reporting centers have a wide appeal to policymakers. They can be touted as "tough" programs given their concern for public safety issues and their attention to treatment concerns. It is the combination of supervision with the services which makes day reporting centers stand out from other community corrections programs.

Recommendations

The implementation of any correctional initiative must include attention to certain principles of development. The concept must be fully developed, the target population clearly identified, and adequate resources secured. In identifying the target population, care must be taken to ensure that it is realistic—in other words, that it exists in numbers sufficient to warrant a program—and that the program design meets the particular needs of the target group.

The program must be marketed, support must be developed, and provisions must be made for continued quality assurance. Program evaluation is an especially important component for new and innovative efforts to demonstrate to those involved, as well as to the general public, that it does indeed meet its intended goals. This is a weak area of day reporting centers. There has been no major evaluation of the centers. Perhaps there are completed studies of an individual program, but these have not been widely publicized. We need sound research to back up our anecdotal confidence that day reporting centers are effective community correctional programs.

The informal results on day reporting centers indicate an exciting opportunity to create truly viable alternatives to traditional methods of offender supervision. With limited resources, continued crowding, and public outcry, this type of intermediate sanction option incorporated into the range of available sanctions can help to effectively and efficiently meet the needs of criminal justice systems.

References

Mair, George. 1988. *Probation Day Centres.* Home Office Research Study 100. London: Her Majesty's Stationery Office.

Crime and Justice Foundation and Northeastern University. 1988. *Evaluation of the Hampden County Day Reporting Center.* Boston, Mass.: Crime and Justice Foundation and Northeastern University.

National Institute of Justice. 1995. *Issues and Practices: Day Reporting Centers,* Volume 1. Washington, D.C.: National Institute of Justice.

12

Examining a Network of Alternatives: Reducing Jail Populations

Neil E. Dorsey

Director
Community Services Program
Howard County Sheriff's Office
Ellicott City, Maryland

The public wants to lock up the bad guys, put the drug dealers away, and get the drunk drivers off the streets. The courts use jails to remove offenders and, in some cases, to treat them. In addition, we now have the deinstitutionalization phenomenon that has caught the community unprepared to deal with the institutional release of persons who require specialized treatment. The American Jail Association devoted an entire issue of its magazine, *American Jails* (November-December, 1995), to these special management inmates in an effort to address this growing population. In Maryland, there are more than 21,000 state inmates and 9,000 people in local jails. The Bureau of Justice Statistics reports that local jails hosted 484,000 adults in 1994 and 5.1 million people were in jail or prison, or on probation or parole at year-end 1994, nearly 2.7 percent of all adult residents in the United States. There is a real problem facing us in corrections: What do we do with all these offenders?

Why is there the need for alternatives? The reasons are simple: It is expensive to lock people up; jails are crowded; and perhaps people can be changed without going to jail and not endanger the public. The public may want to lock people up, but the cost is so high that in Maryland, the Governor proposed that no funding be allocated for state prison construction for the next five years. A recent study reported in *Corrections Today* (Veneziano and Fichter 1995) dealing with the public attitude toward community-based corrections shows that there are misconceptions about the leniency of the criminal justice system. The lack of knowledge about alternatives may be a reason that the community resists acceptance of these programs. What will happen to the offenders who are arrested? What will the courts do with these offenders?

We can see some of the answers to these questions in the beginnings of pretrial programs in common law, where it was possible "to issue a summons instead of a warrant for arrest for the commission of any offense, even a felony . . ." (Gavin 1977). Alternatives such as work release, third-party release programs, pretrial release, treatment assessment screening centers, and other programs have been with us for many years. What is different now is the public's view of alternatives. They want their safety preserved more efficiently and effectively. How do we as local correctional professionals achieve this goal and still keep our jobs?

As with all programs, the services to be offered must be based on the needs of the inmate population and the public. There are many factors to consider before developing an alternative: Who is in your jail? Do you house short-term offenders for driving while intoxicated, nonsupport, or property crimes? Are major offenders in your jail because your state's department of corrections is crowded? How many males, females, first offenders, second offenders, or pretrial detainees do you have in your jail? What is the average length of a stay for a sentenced offender? What is the average length of a stay before adjudication? Are there existing alternative programs in your community? You cannot design a program without knowing who is going into it and what you expect to get out of it. To help in the planning process, see Drapkin, *Developing Policies and Procedures for Jails: A Step-By-Step Guide.*

One of the problems faced in local corrections is that many members of the criminal justice system, elected officials, and the public think they know how to run the jail. They can decide not to fund state prison construction programs, but can they design the programs to handle the offender population in your community? They know that implementing an electronic monitoring program will reduce the jail population and save money. Or will it? The common expression we would read about or hear from the public was a need for alternative sentencing. Now the call has gone out for intermediate sanctions. We can only invent so many different alternatives or intermediate sanctions. The key to any of these programs is proper planning and full cooperation of all the members of the criminal justice system and the public.

Designing the Program

Before jumping on the bandwagon, we must determine what the problem is and design the program based on the problem. The local jails now are faced with a number of special needs offenders: those with tuberculosis or AIDS, the developmentally disabled, and the mentally ill. How these new programs impact the problem should be a major consideration throughout the planning process. Do not try to solve the problem before you know that you have a problem. What will the criteria be for placement in your alternative program? What type of offenders will the public allow into the program? Will the prosecutor allow drug dealers or Driving While Intoxicated offenders on home detention or work release? Will the courts sentence offenders to the alternatives?

After looking at the program design, examine the cost of the alternatives compared to the jail costs. Programs must be staffed. You will need an office and equipment. In Montgomery County, Maryland, the cost of starting a pretrial program in the late 1980s was $850,000. It may be years before the effects on the jail population are seen. What happens if the jail population grows or stays the same? To determine how well the program is working, it must be evaluated based on its initial goals.

A word of caution: Take a look at other operating programs and see how they did it and what problems were identified. Do not let the budget staff or elected officials set your goals without them knowing the potential problems of their "suggestions" or mandates. We do not know of any jurisdiction with a pretrial services program where the jail population decreased based solely on the pretrial program. However, this does not mean pretrial programs will not have a positive effect on the jail population or public safety. The goal of the program may be to slow down the flow of offenders or have them released to a less costly community program at an earlier date. When you design your program, develop realistic goals, a solid budget, and plan for staffing. Learn from the experience of others. You must be able to show that the new program will have a significant impact on the jail population or community and that it will achieve a cost benefit for the criminal justice system. Community-based programs should cost less than institutional programs. To be successful, you must have researched the issue and show both that you have a problem and that the new program will address the problem. New programs could widen the net of offenders with whom you work, thus having an opposite effect on the problem you are trying to solve. Do not forget to set up an evaluation plan for the program. You must be able to show that your new program is meeting its goals.

Now that you have done the proper planning that prevents poor programs, what are the alternatives? Diversion programs can take place at two levels: before the person gets to jail and after he or she is received into the institution. The goals of these programs are to reduce the jail population, or at least make the placement in the jail appropriate for the crime and the individual offender, and to protect the public.

Pretrial Diversion

Traditional pretrial diversion programs can be operated by the local correctional department, the prosecutor, a third-party organization, or a private agency. In "Instead of Jail: Pre- and Post-trial Alternatives to Jail Incarceration," Gavin (1977) discusses pretrial programs, summonses and citations, and post-booking release programs. Alternatives are not new, as this nearly twenty-year-old publication shows. Among the pretrial programs covered in this publication is the well organized Manhattan Bail Project started by the Vera Foundation in 1961 in New York City. Similar programs also are reviewed. They usually involve some form of screening, which consists of verifying the offender's address, prior record, community ties, and employment. Programs based on this limited information release offenders back to the streets. In recent years, drug screens have become a vital part of the screening procedures. In Prince George's and Montgomery counties in Maryland, the collection of drug information is a new part of the original program concept of pretrial diversion programs started years ago. This information can be used in developing a release plan.

A number of these pretrial diversion programs provide supervision of the offender in the community. This ensures that offenders get to court and are provided treatment that may prevent them from returning to crime. A pretrial services program also can work with those offenders who are not diverted prior to being placed in jail. A pretrial unit can review those offenders placed in jail to assist in contacting relatives or friends who may be able to pay for a bond or be willing to have the person released to their custody. Offenders may need only to have their residency or work history verified to be released. A pretrial unit can do this, report to the court, and the court can release the offender with conditions. The offender is out of jail and supervised, and there is a cost savings to the public.

In 1975, the Montgomery County Detention Center received a Law Enforcement Assistance Administration (LEAA) grant to start an intake unit, whose goals were to remove from jails those individuals who could be better served by other community resources and to assist them in exploring the resources available to gain release on a bond. The intake staff did the screening, and the courts based their decision on accurate information. Those offenders not seen as dangerous did not take up jail beds (Gunster-Kirby 1980). A pretrial program can develop a more involved release plan to present to the courts, one that provides increased information and offers community supervision. An added benefit of a pretrial services program is the increased amount of information provided to the jail staff on those offenders who are not released. This information can be the basis for classification of these offenders.

A program started by a number of jurisdictions in the 1970s was the use of community alternatives or work service programs instead of jail time. These programs have grown to include pretrial offenders, with the courts using them in place of fines, as part of active probation and in lieu of weekend sentences. In Maryland, alternative community service provides the pretrial offender and selected sentenced offenders the opportunity to do community work rather than go through a court hearing. The number of court hearings is reduced; police do not have to go to court; parole and probation agents do not have to deal with minor offenders; and the criminal justice system can deal with the major issues before them.

The criterion for selection into the program can be developed in cooperation with the prosecutor, police, and department that will be operating the program. In Maryland, the basic guidelines have been placed into the Maryland Annotated Code (Article 27 Section 726A). The offender is screened by a caseworker prior to the first court appearance or after a sentencing hearing.

A community advisory board is one method of developing the selection criteria and community support for the program. On completion of the community service, the caseworker provides a report to the court or probation agent. The case may be dismissed in pretrial cases. The offenders may be able to have their records expunged after completion of the community work in pretrial cases. One Maryland program helps offenders expunge their records. Community service programs in the larger counties in Maryland averaged more than 1,400 clients annually. They provide thousands of hours of community-work to nonprofit, state, and county agencies. A community service program in Montgomery County, Maryland is also part of two treatment programs for substance abusers who are being diverted from incarceration. Staffing is the only cost, and the returns are many hours of service. Additional benefits to the criminal justice system are that court time and costs are reduced, treatment is provided, and there is immediate punishment to the offender.

Diverting Sentenced Offenders

The courts and the public believe that something will happen to the offender in jail, that some change for the better will occur and, at least, the offender will be off the street. Local correctional professionals also want to reduce jail populations since no one wants to build new jails. How can we accomplish these goals with a sentenced inmate? We can plan and develop programs, ranging from the traditional work release programs to the newer home detention programs that can address the different offender's needs.

A National Institute of Justice research brief, "Systemwide Strategies to Alleviate Jail Crowding," covers a number of the traditional diversion programs. This report contains information about programs such as work release, case screening, citation release, bail setting, and others. A recent development in alternatives has been the use of electronic monitoring and home detention. There have been a number of articles and ongoing studies on the use of home detention. At the November 1990 meeting of the Maryland Criminal Justice Association, Anthony Travisono, former executive director of the American Correctional Association, stated that there were about 7,000 offenders in these programs nationwide. These numbers have increased since 1990 as the use of electronic monitoring as an alternative becomes more accepted by the public. The programs have changed as we gain experience in working with the offenders and redefine program goals based on the changing needs of the community.

These programs offer an alternative to jail for the nonviolent offender. Many ask, why lock up these offenders? Can a person pay off his or her nonsupport in jail? Can the Driving While Intoxicated offender get treatment in jail? Perhaps these offenders can achieve more in the community. What about the pregnant offender, the inmate on dialysis, or even the offender with active AIDS? The community is more equipped than the local jail to treat these offenders. Public safety most likely will not be endangered, and jails will save at least $50 to $75 per day. The types of offenders listed here are only a small number of offenders now in our jails who might be served better in a community alternative sanction. This is why it is so important to do the research on who is in your jail and why they are there.

Work release, prerelease, and day treatment programs have provided viable alternatives for many jurisdictions. Work release is an excellent method for the jurisdiction to recoup some of the costs of running the program. It can range in scope from employers simply allowing individuals to return to their jobs, to programs that provide job placement, career counseling, and on-site supervision. The community must select the type of program and services they want to provide.

The day reporting center is one new alternative that is piquing the interest of corrections professionals. Described as "a hybrid of intensive supervision, house arrest, and early release," the day reporting center began in England and was started in the United States in Springfield, Massachusetts, in 1986 (Williams 1990). In this program, the inmate is out of jail but reports to the day reporting center each day, where medical services, counseling, job training, and educational programs are offered. The National Institute of Justice publication *Day Reporting Centers for Criminal Offenders* (1990) provides further information, as does the National Institute of Corrections Jail Center and the National Institute of Corrections Information Center.

A recent expansion of the community service alternative program is for offenders sentenced to weekends in jail to be given community service in place of the jail sentence. This program can work either as an alternative to serving the actual weekends or if the offender is released during the day, Saturday and/or Sunday, to do community service, returning to the jail that night. A typical weekend prisoner does nothing but take up space and cost the jail money, so why not work them?

CART Program

Another program concept is the Community Accountability and Rehabilitative Treatment Program (CART) implemented by the Montgomery County, Maryland, Department of Correction and Rehabilitation, Community Correctional Services Division. This program combines the concepts of home detention, work release, and diversion. The services depend on the needs of the offender. Typically, when offenders are sentenced to the Montgomery County Department of Correction and Rehabilitation, they are screened by the

Community Corrections Division for possible transfer to the Pre-release Center. This screening can take place before sentencing or after the offenders are in the Detention Center.

Offenders then complete two-to-four months at the Pre-release Center, where they work in the community and are involved in a treatment program. After meeting their prerelease obligations, offenders become eligible for the CART program and are allowed to live at home. However, they are now in an electronic monitoring program and have caseworker visits. There is counseling for the participants and their community sponsors. The combination of treatment and supervision gives this program an opportunity to have a powerful and positive impact on offenders and their families. This program provides transitional release planning and supportive services.

Begun in May 1990, the CART program is an extension of the community correctional system in Montgomery County. The offender flows through the system, from detention to prerelease to CART, based on set criteria aimed at changing the offender and protecting the public. Initial results showed very few revocations. The CART program is an example of a community looking at a jail population problem and deciding on an alternative. The criminal justice system, the public, and elected officials all are involved in this program, which reflects the needs of the jurisdiction.

Determine Which Programs Work for You

Only proper planning, implementation, and evaluation can determine which programs work for you. Jail populations are growing and changing, tax dollars are tight, and changes must be made. Alternatives cannot work without the total cooperation of all the players. Designing a program that the courts, prosecutors, or public does not accept or agree to is a waste of time and money. In the 1990s, the issue of funding also has impacted alternative programs. In Maryland, one county closed down the work release center, and the state closed what was described as a successful juvenile boot camp due to funding issues. There are also two local substance abuse/Driving While Intoxicated programs that have either been closed or greatly reduced because offenders were not sentenced to these alternatives. A similar program in Maryland also is suffering from a lack of clients. The courts, prosecutors, and public say they want these alternatives, but why do they fail to achieve the goals set out for them or have their funds slashed? Corrections cannot solve the problems of crowding and crime alone. We must look at the total system.

Statements made during the years of the Law Enforcement Assistance Administration referred to the criminal justice system as an "unsystem." Twenty-five years later we are still this "unsystem" trying to solve all its problems as individuals. It cannot be done. The immediate problems are crowded jails and a lack of resources. We must determine who are in the jails, how long they stay, why they are there, and then design a program to get them out or offer the opportunity for change. American University offered a course a number of years ago called "Innovations in Corrections." The instructor stated that there has not been an innovative program in corrections in years. We said that twenty-five years ago and we still believe it. The only changes in programs in recent years are the demand for alternatives and redesigned existing programs to meet the new needs of the community.

Alternatives can provide some of the answers to our crowded jails, but we must work with the total community to achieve our goals. We must educate the public about alternatives, about who is really in the jail, and hope this will change the community's view toward the criminal justice system and alternative sanctions. This is our challenge as we move into the twenty-first century.

References

American Jail Association. 1995. *American Jails*. November-December.

Drapkin, Martin. 1996. *Developing Policies and Procedures for Jails: A Step-By-Step Guide*. Lanham, MD: American Correctional Association.

Gavin, John J. 1977. Instead of Jail: Pre- and Post-trial Alternatives to Jail Incarceration. In *Alternatives to Pretrial Detention*. Washington, D.C.: United States Department of Justice, Law Enforcement Assistant Administration.

Gunster-Kirby, Claire. 1980. Intake Unit. Boulder, Colorado: National Institute of Corrections Jail Center.

National Institute of Justice. 1987. Systemwide Strategies to Alleviate Jail Crowding. Washington, D.C.: National Institute of Justice.

———. 1990. *Day Reporting Centers for Criminal Offenders*. Washington, D.C.: National Institute of Justice.

Veneziano, Carol, and Michael Fichter. 1995. Attitudes Examined Toward Community-based Corrections. *Corrections Today*. December.

Williams, Susan Darst. 1990. The Invisible Day Reporting Centers. *Corrections Compendium*. 15(7):3-7.

13

Innovative Alternatives: The Canadian Experience

Brendan Reynolds

Corporate Advisor
Intergovernmental Affairs
Correctional Service of Canada
Ottawa, Canada

The Correctional Service of Canada's mission is to protect society by encouraging and assisting offenders to become law-abiding citizens while exercising reasonable, safe, secure, and humane control. We believe the public is best protected by the safe reintegration of offenders into society. Finding the right balance between the two elements of assistance and control is at the heart of good correctional practice. There is no fixed formula for achieving this balance. We must be constantly innovative and open to new concepts and approaches.

We also need innovative responses to political and economic pressures. The old ways of managing corrections may not work as well with tight budgets and public discontent with the justice system's handling of crime problems. As in other Western countries, the reality of diminishing public resources is forcing us to become more efficient managers. But it is no longer just a matter of doing more with less, since downsized work forces already may be stretched to the limits of their capacity. What is apparent is that we have to be smarter, more results-oriented, and more creative.

The Correctional Service of Canada's determination to meet these challenges has unleashed a significant amount of creative energy within the organization, but this energy will dissipate if it is not harnessed and directed toward a clear purpose. For this reason, having a strategic focus for corrections is so important.

The Correctional Service of Canada, like most organizations, has had a formal strategic planning process for some time. This has enabled us to prioritize our medium-term goals. These priorities are reflected in our corporate objectives, which provide a framework for deciding what specific activities we will undertake. They also challenge us to think innovatively about problems and their solutions.

One of our primary goals is to balance incarceration and community-based corrections. At present, our incarcerated federal population is about 15,000, compared with about 9,500 on some form of conditional release in the community.

We believe that we can improve that ratio with more aggressive case planing for offenders who have reached parole eligibility and can be managed safely in the community. At the same time, we recognize the need to maintain secure custody of high-risk offenders who have a continuing potential for violence.

Our efforts to strengthen our community operations are not solely based on saving money, although the relatively high expense of keeping offenders in institutions is obviously an important consideration. It costs us more than $50,000 a year to incarcerate an inmate, compared with roughly $10,000 to supervise that individual in the community. Nevertheless, any cost reduction achieved by releasing more offenders earlier would be a false economy if public safety were compromised in the process. Our belief in community corrections is tempered by that knowledge. We know we have to be able to demonstrate the effectiveness of our release programs through solid evidence of their impact on reducing recidivism.

Some of that evidence is now beginning to surface. Our research division recently produced a study tracking the recidivism of offenders over two-and-a half years, from 1990 to 1992. The study found that although the number of federal offenders under community supervision during this period had increased by 13 percent, the recidivism rate had not gone up, and in fact had shown an overall decline. Admittedly, this is only a short-term study, but it does give encouraging signs that our investment in community programming is starting to pay off.

Part of the basis for pursuing a more aggressive approach to community corrections lies in the establishment of a sound system of measuring and managing risk effectively. Much of our effort has gone into devising reliable risk-assessment tools and prediction models that reflect state-of-the-art research.

The result of this research is a comprehensive system that treats risk as dynamic and variable throughout the offender's sentence and allows us to decide what type of intervention is needed at what stage. A few years ago we developed and implemented a risk/needs scale specifically for use in supervising offenders in the community. Subsequent to that we developed a comprehensive approach to offender evaluation at the start of their sentences.

Developing a front-end assessment process is complicated because it takes in and weighs information from a multitude of sources, from police reports to psychological tests, to create a profile of the newly admitted offender and identify the main factors that appear to contribute to criminal behavior. This helps determine what programs, treatment, education, and training would be likely to have a positive effect within an individualized correctional treatment plan.

Through other initiatives, we have tried to get a better grasp of some of the specific components of risk, such as substance abuse. One recent innovation is a computerized lifestyle assessment that examines data related to an offender's social situation, work history, and use of leisure time to find patterns of substance abuse associated with criminal activity.

With good methods for assessing risk and needs, we can direct programming appropriately and avoid spending precious resources in areas less likely to produce the results we want. In our correctional strategy, we have developed an approach that delivers certain core programs, such as literacy and cognitive skills courses, to all offenders, while tailoring specialized therapeutic regimens to meet the needs of particular groups such as sex offenders.

We also are working with innovative concepts in designing our institutions, recognizing that physical surroundings play a large part in determining the quality of staff-inmate interaction and can either help or hinder a program's effectiveness. In 1992, the Correctional Service of Canada completed a large-scale reconstruction of the inmate housing areas at William Head Institution in British Columbia. We replaced the old cell blocks with clusters of eight five-bedroom houses grouped around a "neighborhood center" that provides both program space and services ranging from laundry to library. The new design, with its noninstitutional look, is meant to approximate the conditions the inmates will find in the community and will encourage them to become more independent and assume greater responsibility for their own lives.

This same philosophy of normalization underlies the residential arrangements in the five regional centers for federal female offenders that have replaced the sixty-year-old Prison for Women in Kingston, Ontario. These facilities, one of which is a healing lodge for aboriginal women, range in size from thirty to seventy-six beds and incorporate design features specific to the needs of women. The residential units afford considerable personal privacy, with small numbers of inmates sharing common services such as kitchen, dining and recreation areas. Some houses have sleeping space to accommodate inmates' children while on visits.

Our approach reflects the legislative framework that we now have in place for federal corrections in Canada. Our Corrections and Conditional Release Act recognizes the distinction between less serious offenders, who should be able to return safely to the community early in their sentences, and violent offenders, who may require longer periods of incarceration.

The legislation provides an accelerated review process for the first group that, in many cases, results automatically in their release under supervision at no later than a third of their sentence. This enables us to focus on the second, more difficult group and provide them with the more intensive security and programming needed to reduce their risk to assumable levels.

The legislation provides an ample range of tools for managing the safe release of offenders according to their needs at various points in the sentence. Escorted and unescorted temporary absences, work releases, day parole and full parole can be linked together into a coherent plan that enables us to test the offender's capacity for gradually increased responsibility.

At the same time, we realize we cannot undertake these innovations on our own. We must rely on strong cooperative ties with our partners in the criminal justice system and the community to ensure that all available resources are mobilized. This demands new ways of thinking as we try to break down traditional territoriality that has long affected how the criminal justice system operates. For example, historically, the corrections and mental health systems in Canada have cooperated only minimally with each other. Today, however, they find themselves faced with a common clientele who do not respect tidy jurisdictional boundaries. The past lack of coordination has sometimes had disastrous consequences involving released offenders in the community. We are now in the process of establishing protocols among federal and provincial corrections and the provincial mental health ministries to allow us to share individual case records and research related to the treatment of mentally disordered offenders, as well as other expertise and technological innovations.

In the Correctional Service of Canada's Atlantic region, we are making impressive headway in establishing cooperative ties with the mental health and corrections systems of the province of Nova Scotia. Memoranda of understanding have been developed, allowing us to establish, along with the province, community assessment and treatment programs for sex offenders and mentally disordered offenders who are on conditional release. Similarly encouraging initiatives toward joint service delivery to these groups also are occurring in British Columbia.

Finding and demonstrating programming that works remains one of our greatest challenges as we approach the year 2000. We have amassed considerable knowledge about the effectiveness of various therapeutic models in treating criminal behavior. Much more needs to be done. We are still trying to unravel psycho-social causes of crime in an attempt to build more reliable instruments for predicting recidivism risk in individual cases and for knowing what mix of interventions will reduce that risk.

At the same time, future breakthroughs depend on having a solid foundation to measure and evaluate what we have now. Our information systems and evaluation specialists are heavily engaged in developing the data capture and analysis capabilities needed for that to happen.

As we learn about the effectiveness of our programs, we have a duty to share that knowledge with the criminal justice community and with the public at large. We are grappling with the challenge of creating new and better networks of communication and consultation, of breaking down the barriers of misinformation that for too long have frustrated attempts to establish the credibility and legitimacy of corrections work. We can point to some successes, despite the general public's "get tough on crime" mood.

In short, we have to be confident about what works, and we have to inform those whose help is essential to implementing effective correctional practices. This will demand a flexible approach, an ability to wean ourselves from reliance on rigid hierarchies, and an openness to forming strategic alliances with new and perhaps unexpected partners.

We must build innovation—managed responsibly and with proper regard for accountability—into our organizations. We owe the public, the offenders in our charge, our employees, and ourselves nothing less.

14

The Development of a Community Corrections Literacy Program*

Cary W. Harkaway

Deputy Director
Multnomah County Department of Community Corrections
Portland, Oregon

This paper describes the development of the Donald H. Londer Center for Learning (CFL), a literacy program that targets adult offenders under probation and parole supervision of the Multnomah County Department of Community Corrections (DCC) in Portland, Oregon. The first part of the paper offers a new perspective for understanding such endeavors. The next three sections discuss needs assessment data, program development and implementation, and evaluation issues. The last section discusses the emerging role of the program as a catalyst for new developments.

An Evolutionary Perspective

Why is the relationship between corrections and education so strong? We may enhance our understanding of that synergism by approaching correctional education from an evolutionary perspective. Consider this statement: In providing literacy training for adult offenders, we are committed to programming designed to restore our clients' evolutionary birthrights. The objectives of correctional programs usually are defined in terms of community protection or offender rehabilitation. Educational programs typically are defined by objectives related to the mastery of specific competencies or skills. What does either set of objectives have to do with evolutionary birthrights? In *Origins: What*

*This paper expands on an earlier paper presented to the American Correctional Association Winter Conference in Orlando, Florida in January 1994. The author wishes to thank Cynthia Stadel, coordinator of the Donald H. Londer Center for Learning for her assistance in preparing both papers. The program described herein was originally supported by U. S. Department of Education grant number V255A30013 awarded under the Functional Literacy for State and Local Prisoners Program in December 1992.

New Discoveries Reveal About the Emergence of Our Species and Its Possible Future (1977, p. 51), Richard Leakey and Roger Lewin wrote that:

> The reason the higher primates tend to be social animals is that group living offers the opportunity for prolonged learning during childhood; and learning is a pastime in which primates engage far more than any other animal. Learning is a pastime with a purpose, however—namely to equip individuals in a group with a more effective knowledge of the environment in which they must survive. Greater knowledge implies a greater chance of survival—which is what evolution is all about.

Building on that grand statement, we could say that to be Homo sapiens is (1) to live in a society that values education, (2) to be educated, and (3) to use that education to enhance the quality of one's life. That is our evolutionary birthright. Quite simply, we have clients who, for a number of reasons, missed their best opportunities for learning and for success in their environments. We can give them another chance. We can restore their evolutionary birthright.

Surely, though, the Multnomah County Department of Community Corrections is not in the business of restoring the evolutionary birthrights of convicted felons. Or are we? In its broadest context, correctional education is the process by which offenders under community or institutional supervision are taught the skills and competencies which they need to survive and be successful as they are reintegrated in their communities. In complex societies, survival and success require a wide range of subsistence skills. Early peoples needed to learn to hunt cooperatively and convert the resources at hand into food, clothing, shelter, and tools. Our clients need to develop the basic literacy, computation, communication, and problem-solving skills which are essential in today's workplace. An evolutionary perspective provides a framework for understanding and appreciating the necessity for correctional education. Without our intervention, our clients still will struggle for survival and success. However, their opportunities and resources will be limited by their skills and competencies. Many will continue to compensate for their deficiencies by victimizing others or using drugs. The result will be high rates of recidivism. Clearly, providing literacy and basic education programs for offenders is sound correctional policy. A review of needs assessment data will support that statement.

Needs Assessment

The Basic Adult Skills Inventory System (BASIS), routinely administered to inmates, documents the need for literacy programs for corrections' clients in Oregon. This standardized test was developed in Oregon to complement the widely used Comprehensive Adult Student Assessment System (CASAS). BASIS determines general level of functioning in reading and computation. CASAS measures competency in discrete life skills, such as consumer economics and health, across several levels of difficulty. In November 1992, 42 percent scored below a ninth-grade (pre-GED) reading level and 83 percent scored below a ninth-grade (pre-GED) math level (Office of Community College Services 1992). That information was part of the justification for the program. More powerful support is based on the relationships between educational deficits and other measurable factors. Data supports the generally accepted correlation between educational attainment and employment status. The Department of Community Corrections published a client needs assessment in 1989, based on a 20 percent random sample of approximately 6,500 felony cases under probation or parole supervision (Harkaway 1989). The department discovered the following:

1. Overall, 35 percent of the offenders under community supervision were unemployed, a rate which has held steady in recent years while the unemployment rate for the Portland Metropolitan Area has varied between 5 percent and 7 percent.

2. The unemployment rate of offenders with less than a ninth-grade education was more than twice the rate of those who graduated from high school (55 percent versus 23 percent).

3. The unemployment rate of offenders with identified drug abuse problems was more than twice the rate of those without such problems (54 percent versus 23 percent). More recent data is consistent with the 1989 findings. In 1994, approximately 57 percent of the participants in a local Drug Diversion Program were unemployed at enrollment.

How should the department have responded to this data? The following assumptions served as guidelines:

1. The problem areas identified in needs assessments are related and compound each other.

2. The most effective interventions are those which integrate program components and are responsive to priority risk and need factors (programmatic integration).

3. Service delivery systems also must integrate the roles of offender supervision, treatment, and sanctions (systems integration).

4. Literacy and basic education are prerequisites for productive, self-sufficient lifestyles.

Clearly, an unacceptably high percentage of our parolees and probationers is limited by both educational and employment deficits. The need for literacy and adult education intervention in corrections' populations is particularly significant. The Board of Directors of the National Council on Crime and Delinquency (1993) noted the connection between failure in school and drug addiction, adult criminality, lower median income, and welfare dependency. Additionally, unemployment has been correlated with recidivism in a number of risk assessment studies (Travis 1990).

Program Development and Implementation

The Multnomah County Department of Community Corrections began working with a group of concerned education, employment, and criminal justice leaders in 1991 with the goal of establishing a literacy, adult education, and life skills program for offenders. Several members of this group visited jurisdictions that had made substantial commitments to literacy for corrections' populations. The group concluded that an integrated learning system that was designed for adults offered the most cost-effective opportunity to reach clients who had not been reached in our public schools. We developed an integrated learning system which involves computer-assisted instruction, a wide-ranging, flexible curriculum, and individually paced lessons. This planning effort coincided with the announcement of the United States Department of Education's Functional Literacy for State and Local Prisoners' Program. Our Department of Corrections was awarded a grant under that program in December 1992 to implement a literacy program for community corrections' clients.

Continuity in Community and Institutional Programming

Terms of incarceration are often brief. Many offenders will alternate between custodial and community supervision. One of the objectives of the planning process was to develop an integrated literacy, adult education, and life skills program that is available to offenders on probation, in correctional facilities, and on parole. This would allow offenders to continue their educations with minimal disruption or repetition as they move between state and county supervision and custody. An Oregon statute enacted in 1989 requires mandatory literacy programs for inmates who are below a functional literacy level. In response to the statute, the state was planning to install an integrated learning system in their prisons. Because close to half of all prison releasees return to Multnomah County, it made sense for the Oregon Department of Corrections and the Multnomah County Department of Community Corrections to collaborate in purchasing a system. Staff from both agencies visited sites where different integrated learning systems were operating, and decided on the most suitable system for state and county needs. The Invest system, developed by Jostens Learning Corporation, was rated highest by staff.

The intent of state and county corrections agencies has been to provide continuity in programming between community and institutional corrections. Literacy services proved to be an excellent example of cooperative prison-community program development. Progress also is being made in the areas of drug treatment and life skills training.

Educational Model

To be effective with the target population, the program must avoid the conditions that were associated with their prior educational failures. It must provide nontraditional learning methods and environments, individually prescribed and individually paced lessons, relevant content reflecting adult experiences, practical applications of literacy skills, and small sequential learning increments designed to guarantee some successes for all participants. The program design included instruction in life skills and preemployment training. To accomplish key objectives in those areas, we implemented group and workshop formats to supplement the instruction that the Invest system provides. Program development staff visited a neighboring state where a literacy program operates with links to job readiness and job placement components. Staff concluded that the observed links were merely sequential program opportunities rather than integrated components. Our intention was to develop an integrated program in which groups and workshops are used to reinforce some of the computer-based instruction by providing practical applications for the lessons. We developed applications in consumer economics, community resources, health, job search skills, and career planning. A wide range of life skills applications are now available.

Implementation Timeline

In February 1993, about two months after the grant award, the department contracted for program evaluation services. We wanted to have the evaluator in place early to improve database design and to assess program development and implementation. We negotiated an agreement with Portland Community College to take advantage of their pool of instructional support staff. The relationship with the college creates a flexible staffing capability which allows for response to emerging client needs. This relationship also connects the Multonomah County Department of Community Corrections with the largest provider of adult education services in the state.

In June 1993, state and county staffs participated in joint training on the Invest, conducted by Jostens Learning Corporation under the terms of the purchase agreements. Oregon's Office of Community College Services provide additional staff training in the use of the BASIS/CASAS assessment system and in adult education issues.

We completed hardware and software installation and testing in August 1993 and enrolled the first participants in September 1993. Later that month, we celebrated the opening of the program in a well-publicized event, which was attended by state and local officials and community leaders, including most of those who were involved in the original planning process more than two years earlier. The program was officially named the Donald H. Londer Center for Learning (CFL), after the Presiding Circuit Court Judge who was an early and effective advocate for literacy training.

All of the Center for Learning's initial clients were involved in either contracted residential drug-treatment programs or the Multnomah County Restitution Center (a residential facility operated by the sheriff) because of a federal grant requirement that a "custodial" population be targeted. However, the terms of our grant allowed for an expansion of the program to the general probation and parole population after services were implemented for the residential programs. That expansion began in February 1994. In February 1996, about half of the participants were nonresidential probationers or parolees. With both the original residential population and the expanded target population, the program had to consider some implementation issues differently from similar programs operated in jail or prison settings.

During the first few years of operation, the Center for Learning had to satisfy concerns related to program demand and results. Program accessibility was the key to meeting those concerns. Making the program accessible meant using flexible scheduling, employing open enrollment, offering on-site General Education Development testing, and paying attention to special learning needs. Staff realized that educational impact depended on accessibility which was necessary to assure a reasonable rate of retention.

Scheduling

Residential program participants and those who are employed typically have full daily schedules. The Center for Learning, therefore, had to provide early morning, evening, and weekend sessions. To further accommodate the residential programs, and to maximize the integration of literacy and adult basic education with the department's other treatment and sanction interventions, staff from the Center for Learning agreed to locate three of the twenty learning system computer stations off-site at two contract drug-treatment facilities and the Restitution Center. This provided additional on-line hours for participants to supplement their work at the Center for Learning.

Information provided by the managers of similar programs in other jurisdictions indicates that sixty hours of instruction is the minimum time necessary to achieve significant results. Flexible hours of operation and the off-site stations will increase the ability of target populations to access the program, but staff expected that it would take Center for Learning participants longer to log sixty hours than participants in similar jail or prison programs. In fact, that proved to be the case. Educational interventions in jails and prisons have some advantages in scheduling compared to community-based programs, because client transportation is not an issue (though other logistical problems may be significant) and because many correctional facilities have long histories of providing such services. In those facilities, a baseline expectation of inmate and facility commitment already has been established. In Multnomah County, literacy and adult education was a new program in the array of interventions offered for parolees and probationers.

Cohort-based Instruction Versus Open Enrollment

To serve the wider population of probationers and parolees, in addition to the initial residential population, the program had to change from cohort-based instruction to a more varied mix of clients with different enrollment dates. For initial clients, specific time periods were worked out with each participating residential program. That resulted in cohorts being enrolled and going through assessment, orientation, and instruction together. The implementation evaluation (Finigan 1993), prepared after three months of program operation, noted that working repeatedly with the same cohorts proved to be an instructional and logistical advantage. It allowed for more structured instructional time, which staff have found to be a benefit with the target population. It also made it easier for staff to schedule and deliver the off-line curriculum (groups and workshops).

The cohort advantage disappeared as the program matured. To manage the logistics of open entry and exit, the program began scheduling frequent orientation periods for new referrals to avoid disrupting regular instruction. The group and workshop sessions were modified as independent units, supportive of the on-line curriculum but offered in a rotation which participants can access in any sequence.

The Use of Incentives

The provision of a community-based (as opposed to an institution-based) literacy program led to some discussion about the use of incentives to motivate offenders. Many correctional facilities, including Oregon's state prisons, provide statutorily mandated literacy programs for target populations. Correctional facilities often rely on incentives to help motivate inmates to improve their basic skills. Many institutions pay inmates a wage, allow certain privileges, or award good time credit for an acceptable level of program participation. In our community corrections residential programs, staff were able to mandate participation in the Center for Learning because they have custodial and program responsibility for their clients. However, as the Center for Learning began to serve the general probation and parole population, motivation was expected to be a problem. In a community setting, clients have many more choices and relative freedom in deciding how to spend their time, compared to inmates and residential program participants. The Department of Corrections explored these strategies:

1. Working with the courts and the parole board to make satisfactory participation at the Center for Learning a condition of supervision for offenders who are below a functional level of literacy;

2. Establishing, with court and board support, a "contract" with targeted offenders by which the attainment of specific educational objectives would result in a request for an early termination of supervision; and,

3. Developing an employment assistance component for those who achieve specific educational objectives.

The options involving the court and parole board have been used in a limited number of individual cases rather than systematically. The third strategy, the offer of employment assistance, proved to be a strong incentive after its implementation, but, surprisingly, an incentive which was not often necessary to motivate participants. Program staff found that many participants saw a value in working on their basic skills' deficits as a necessary step toward enhanced earning power, self-improvement, or some other goal. Indeed, early concerns related to demand for the program in the target population proved to be groundless. Probation and parole officers and other community corrections staff found sufficient interest among clients to help the Center for Learning consistently exceed enrollment projections.

Focus on GED

As increasing numbers of participants pursued their General Equivalency Diploma, many experienced some difficulty in arranging to take the tests at the local community college. Cost, transportation, and timing were the main obstacles. In response, the program worked with the Oregon Office of Community College Services to establish itself as a General Eduaction Development testing center. The Department of Corrections set aside funds to cover administrative costs and participant fees. We were able to coordinate participant testing schedules with their academic progress. Attaining the General Equivalency Diploma is a major goal for participants and an achievement that the program sought to celebrate in a special way. The Hon. Donald H. Londer, Presiding Judge of the Multnomah County Circuit Court, suggested that General Equivalency Diploma ceremonies be held in his courtroom with himself as master of ceremonies. Several such "graduations" have been held, and each has been an emotionally rich experience shared by participants, their families, program staff, the court, and a number of community leaders. No doubt having the ceremony in a courtroom has symbolic strength for a population that has not had many positive experiences in court.

Focus on Learning Disabilities

After a few months of operation, program staff realized that the progress of many participants was limited by their learning disabilities. To build a capacity to serve this population, the department contracted with a consultant to assist in the development of a screening instrument to identify participants who may have learning disabilities and to suggest ways to adapt the program to accommodate their learning needs. The screening instrument, administered to 10 to 15 percent of participants, proved to be useful in determining an individual's preferred learning style and strengths. As a result, most accommodations were a matter of using that information in combination with a variety of educational media and environments (written material, verbal material, recorded material, computer instruction, group interaction, one-on-one tutoring, quiet rooms). The screening instrument also enabled staff to identify participants who required testing and diagnosis for learning disabilities prior to establishing a case plan. We made arrangements for such testing with the Pacific University Psychological Service Center. This testing, administered to 1 to 2 percent of participants, has enabled staff to obtain diagnoses of learning disabilities or attention disorders, and to separate those problems from mental health issues.

Program Evaluation

The program evaluator completed an implementation evaluation in December 1993 (Finigan 1993). This report discussed the major issues involved in the early stages of the program, particularly those related to reaching the target population and fine-tuning the integrated learning system hardware and software. The report offered several recommendations and provided an overview of initial client participation. The program enrolled eighty clients in its first three months of operation. All enrolled clients met the criteria of scoring below a pre-General Equivalency Diploma level (below ninth-grade level) in reading or math on the BASIS. However, about 40 percent of them had a General Equivalency Diploma or a high school diploma. That indicated that the BASIS/CASAS system for assessment, with its emphasis on functional competencies, may test for different skills than the Genreal Education Development test or the typical high school curriculum, both of which emphasize academic achievement. Complicating the picture somewhat was the computer-based Invest curriculum, which also tests for academic achievement measured in approximate grade-level equivalents. The National Literacy Act of 1991 defines literacy as "an individual's ability to read, write, and speak in English and compute and solve problems at levels of proficiency necessary to function on the job and in society, to achieve one's goals and develop one's knowledge and potential." That definition is broad enough to support several measures of educational progress, including:

1. BASIS/CASAS assessments since the BASIS scores are used to screen clients for program entry, because statewide BASIS/CASAS data is available for comparison, and because CASAS measures the application of specific competencies in life and work;

2. Jostens Invest measures of approximate grade level equivalency because they appear to be valid measures of academic achievement and because such measures have intrinsic value to participants and to interested citizens;

3. Success in the General Education Development exams because such progress is a necessary link with subsequent employment and educational opportunities; and,

4. Attainment of a specific personal goal requiring an improved level of functioning in basic skills.

The formative evaluation, completed in March 1994 (Finigan 1994a), supported the premise that sixty hours of instruction is a milestone for significant educational impact. Although measurable progress is initially demonstrated at twenty hours, we noted consistent progress of one-to-two grade level equivalents for participants averaging between fifty and sixty hours.

Finigan (1994b) completed an outcome evaluation in November 1994. The outcome study reported on the impact of program participation on a number of measures related to community adjustment,[1] successful supervision, and recidivism. The evaluation compared a treatment group (n=60) which received a minimum of twenty hours of instruction with a comparison group (n=65) which was referred for service and determined eligible, but which received five hours or less of instruction. An analysis of covariance controlling for preexisting differences between the groups produced very positive findings. The treatment group had better overall community adjustment scores, fewer days on abscond status, fewer technical violations, fewer new arrests, and higher earnings. The evaluator cautioned that, although his findings were based on statistically significant differences between the groups, they lack the strength of an experimental design. The evaluation noted that some differences between the groups may be due to client motivation, which was not measured, and that clients who are willing to spend at least twenty hours in instruction may be better motivated toward positive change in other areas of their lives. The evaluator concluded that ". . . it is reasonable to argue that the Literacy Program is itself a motivation enhancing experience for clients and that it is an important part of a constellation of services that motivate an offender toward change" (1994b, p. 24).

The program has continued to monitor its performance on outcome measures. Data for 1994-95 indicated that 57 percent of the 230 participants who left the program mastered at least one grade-level equivalent or one CASAS level, or passed at least one of the five General Equivalency Development tests, or met a specific personal goal requiring basic skills study (such as passing the written driver's test). Of the eighty-eight participants who logged twenty or more hours of instruction, 91 percent achieved one of those measures of success. All twenty participants who logged at least sixty hours achieved one of those measures of success. Although data suggests that program impact could be enhanced if retention rates increased, the department believes that even modest retention rates are commendable, given the limitations that the target population brings to the program.

Program as Catalyst

After operation of the program for about one year, staff identified a need for a strong vocational education component. Preemployment training and job placement services were in place, but affordable training for high-demand occupations was not readily available. Representatives of most of the agencies involved in the initial planning for a literacy program for offenders began meeting again to identify resources that could be applied to the objective of vocational training.

The Private Industry Council, the Oregon Employment Department, and Portland Community College were especially responsive. The Employment Department assigned a counselor to the Center for Learning. With computer access to statewide job listings, this individual is a valuable supplement to the job search and placement assistance funded by the Department of Corrections. The Private Industry Council and the College collaborated in adapting the Skill-Tech training program from a curriculum developed by the Center for Occupational Research and Development in Waco, Texas. The curriculum provides a broad base of technical knowledge in computer applications, technical graphics, applied mathematics, electricity and electronics, mechanical and fluid systems, and quality control. A pilot version of the curriculum indicated its value as preparation for entry-level technical employment or advanced technical training.

The public and private agencies that responded to the need for vocational training have continued to meet as a consortium called "Foundations."

Foundations has leveraged funding and coordinated resources targeting offender education, employment, and support services. The Department of Corrections has worked through Foundations to integrate educational and vocational interventions consistent with the recommendations of a United States Department of Labor report, *What Work Requires of American Schools,* prepared by the Secretary's Commission on Achieving Necessary Skills (SCANS). The report documents the desirability of a confluence of educational objectives and workplace needs. It also identified a core of foundations and competencies which are becoming increasingly critical elements in the preparation of a qualified workforce. Key foundations include functional literacy (reading, writing, mathematics), thinking skills (creative thinking, decision making, problem solving), and personal qualities (responsibility, self-esteem, self-management, and integrity). Competencies include resource and information management, teamwork, system relationships and operations, and technological literacy.

The Department of Corrections realizes that these foundations, skills, and competencies are a requirement for success in many areas of life. As a result, Center for Learning staff have collaborated with staff from other Department of Corrections programs, as well as public and private agencies, to assure that the educational, counseling, life skills, and cognitive interventions offered to offenders throughout the county are supportive of each other and consistent with shared objectives for public safety and workforce development. The department's experience in the development of the Donald H. Londer Center for Learning over the last several years has been of immeasurable value in integrating social service, education, and corrections agencies with shared goals for safe and healthy communities.

Note

[1]A scale of positive adjustment was adopted from one used by Latessa and Vito (1988) in "The Effects of Intensive Supervision on Shock Probationers," *Journal of Criminal Justice,* v. 16, pp. 319-330. The scale used by Finigan included such factors as stable residence, employment status and progress, negative incidents and illegal activities, and participation in self-improvement programs.

References

Finigan, Michael. 1993. *Implementation Evaluation of the Multnomah County Community Corrections Literacy Program for Adult Offenders.* West Linn, Oregon: Northwest Professional Consortium.

———. 1994a. *Formative Evaluation of the Multnomah County Community Corrections Literacy Program for Adult Offenders.* West Linn, Oregon: Northwest Professional Consortium.

———. 1994b. *Outcome Evaluation Report: Multnomah County Community Corrections Literacy Program for Adult Offenders.* West Linn,

Oregon: Northwest Professional Consortium.

Harkaway, Cary W. 1989. *Client Needs Assessment: Planning, Program, and Policy Implications.* Portland, Oregon: Multnomah County Department of Community Corrections.

Leakey, Richard E., and Roger Lewin. 1977. *Origins: What New Discoveries Reveal About the Emergence of Our Species and its Possible Future.* New York: E. P. Dutton.

National Council on Crime and Delinquency. 1993. *Reducing Crime in America: A Pragmatic Approach.* San Francisco, California: National Council on Crime and Delinquency.

Office of Community College Services. 1992. *BASIS Scores for Corrections Clients,* November 1992. Salem, Oregon: Office of Community College Services.

Secretary's Commission on Achieving Necessary Skills. 1991. *What Work Requires of American Schools.* Washington, D.C.: U. S. Department of Labor.

Travis, Lawrence F. 1990. Risk Classification in Probation and Parole: Issues and Trends. Paper presented at the Annual Meeting of the Academy of Criminal Justice Sciences, Denver, Colorado.

Electronic Monitoring

The following essays focus on various facets of electronic monitoring, an important component of community corrections.

Electronic Monitoring: Past, Present, and Future

Annesley K. Schmidt

Community Corrections Specialist
Federal Bureau of Prisons
Washington, D.C.

While electronic monitoring (EM) of offenders has been feasible for about the last ten or fifteen years in the United States, the technology still is evolving and developing. As a result, there are a variety of options available and alternatives to chose from (and as soon as this document is printed, new ones will undoubtedly be developed in addition to those discussed here).

What is Electronic Monitoring?

Electronic monitoring refers to the use of telemetry technology to assist in monitoring the activities of an offender and ensure that the person remains in a specified location during required hours. Usually the offender is in the community and living at home, but electronic monitoring is sometimes used with offenders in halfway houses or correctional facilities. Electronic monitoring currently is being used by sheriffs, police departments, probation and parole departments for adult and juvenile offenders including those on work furloughs, specified sex offenders, those subject to intensive supervision, offenders assigned to work release or work crews, and for some inmates who have had to be released from custody due to population caps or other restrictions on available jail beds.

---

*Mrs. Schmidt is a community corrections specialist with the Federal Bureau of Prisons. She chaired the Standards Subcommittee of the Electronic Monitoring Committee of the International Association of Residential and Community Alternatives (IARCA, now called the International Community Corrections Association) that played a role in the development of the American Correctional Association Standards for Electronic Monitoring. The points of view expressed in this article are her own and do not necessarily reflect the official position of the Bureau of Prisons or the United States Department of Justice.

Almost from the beginning, there was a subcommittee on standards, which this author chaired.

Several early discussions in the standards subcommittee focused on the question: what kind of product should be our goal? Two clear alternatives emerged. The subcommittee could develop standards similar to the American Correctional Association that said, for example, there should be a policy on how violations are handled; or, it could develop what would be called standards but actually were guidelines that would recommend a way to respond to violations. The subcommittee decided to try to develop American Correctional Association-type standards with the intent that they would eventually become part of the American Correctional Association standards programs which is well thought of and well established.

As we looked for applicable standards, we found that many of the American Correctional Association standards were close but not completely applicable. Therefore, it soon became obvious that we would have to write our own. Two things provided a head start: 1) the then-newly written American Correctional Association standards on correctional boot camps, and 2) the Community Justice Coalition of Connecticut, Inc., who generously shared their Community Corrections Standards for Nonresidential Programs[5]. Using these two sources, numerous drafts of the standards were written, revised, edited, and sent out for comment. Then, the process started all over again with more revising, editing, and distribution for comments. The process of developing standards and refining them involved the help and participation of many people. Without all of the assistance and cooperation, the standards never would have been completed.

At the August, 1993 American Correctional Association meeting in Nashville, Linda Connelly and this author met with Hardy Rauch, then Director of Standards and Accreditation, to discuss the process needed to convert our draft into American Correctional Association standards. We then appeared before the Standards and Accreditation Committee to make our case and solicit their support. We also worked with the American Correctional Association Standards and Accreditation staff. One draft was completed in February, 1994, and another in May of that same year. The interactive process continued with a presentation to the Committee on Standards and Accreditation. Finally, Standards for Electronic Monitoring Programs[6] was published in 1995. It is available from the American Correctional Association.

Electronic monitoring appears in a number of settings within the criminal justice system. Electronic monitoring may be operated in conjunction with both adult and juvenile programs that provide community residential services, probation and parole field services, and detention services. Many of these areas already have standards.

The fact that electronic monitoring may be a stand-alone program or may operate as a part of other programs led to an unusual feature of these standards: a standards book for stand-alone programs and a chapter related to electronic monitoring which can be added to any of the other standards when accrediting a program that also offers electronic monitoring.

Now, the standards are being used to accredit electronic monitoring programs, and as part of the American Correctional Association's accreditation process, they will be subject to the continual fine-tuning and refining which is a hallmark of that process. At the same time, we believe that they will be applicable to the next generation of equipment.

Electronic Monitoring at Present

There is at least one electronic monitoring program in each state and in a number of foreign countries. It is safe to estimate that there are at least 20,000 people being electronically monitored on any given day. Over the years, the programmed contact and continuously signaling equipment has become more reliable and less subject to interference and problems. For example, the signal of some early equipment was unaltered if the offender removed it and left it near the receiver-dialer, making it appear as though the offender were home. Now, most types of equipment have tamper-resistant bands so that the signal changes when it is altered or removed. The offender can still attempt to remove the band. However, the central monitoring station will be alerted by a tamper signal.

The developers of equipment and the service providers have enhanced not only the equipment but their offerings. Software now is available not only to monitor the output of the equipment but to provide the user with a variety of case management services. Additionally, the companies can collect certain fees for service through a 900 number telephone service.

The Future of Electronic Monitoring

The development of the next generation of equipment is progressing. There are efforts currently under way to develop affordable new technology for what is being called tracking electronic monitoring (TEM). Tracking electronic monitoring is different from today's electronic monitoring in that it will be used to keep track of offenders as they move around the community, from one location to another. Much like the locating technology that helps locate stolen vehicles, tracking electronic monitoring will help officers keep track of probationers, parolees, or other offender groups in the community and will create a log of each offender's location which developers hope will help detect and apprehend those who commit new crimes. As with the currently available continuously signaling electronic monitoring, tracking electronic monitoring will require significant personnel resources to follow up and/or respond to the information provided by the technology.

Tracking electronic monitoring for use in cities is being developed and just becoming commercially available. There are several approaches emerging. One approach requires the offender to wear a transmitter which will signal periodically like the present transmitter used on continuously signaling equipment. This signal will be received by devices located throughout a specified geographical area on a grid which will allow the offender's specific location within the area to be determined. As the offender moves, the path is plotted and may be compared with an approved route or location.

Other approaches to tracking electronic monitoring would require the offender to have more equipment than can be presently miniaturized. One company's[7] approach has the offender wear an ankle device which is connected to transmitters which signal global positioning satellites and are carried in a fanny pack. The strap connecting the two can be worn unobtrusively under clothing when the offender is moving around the community. When the offender is sitting or sleeping, the fanny pack can be taken off and placed nearby.

Another company[8] has tested prototypes and will soon begin to manufacture a system in which the offender wears a bracelet. The portable tracking device or receiver is separate and programmed so that it must be within a fixed but adjustable distance from the bracelet. The portable tracking device is about the size of a cigar box and can transmit over the telephone lines or the wireless network when the offender is at home and over the wireless network when the offender is moving around the community. The information on offender movements can be reported in real time or stored and transmitted periodically depending on the perceived risk level of the offender.

The National Institute of Justice supported a grant to investigate the technological feasibility of implementing a community-wide electronic monitoring system[9] to locate persons on probation or parole. Their grantee selected a one-half mile square area of downtown Pittsburgh to represent a typical urban environment. Using off-the-shelf equipment, including spread-spectrum receivers, time-of-arrival circuits, and cellular telephones, they formed an experimental area with four base stations. They simulated ankle transmitters within the cell to project the performance characteristics of a full-scale, communitywide, multi-cell tracking system. The researchers concluded that the project had "successfully demonstrated the technical feasibility of locating and tracking a body-worn transmitter in an urban environment using a multi-cellular system of base-station receivers."[10] A follow-up study is proposed in which they will change the configuration of a cell from four-sided to six-sided to improve accuracy and availability of the signal. They also propose to increase the power level of the signal and miniaturize the spread-spectrum transmitter.

Although there are many reasons to hold high hopes for tracking technology, its application is likely to be limited by its cost and by corrections' and law enforcement's ability to respond to the information generated. Suppose tracking electronic monitoring lets us know that a particular offender, who is required to abstain from alcohol, has walked or driven home up Second Street past a liquor store instead of up Third Street as expected or required. To what use will that information be put, if the offender is not late getting home? How are we to intervene to use tracking electronic monitoring as a crime stopper? Will we be subject to increased liability if a monitored offender commits a new crime while we "knew or should have known" where he or she was at all times?

Tracking equipment is described in some literature as "second generation" monitoring equipment. In addition to the features described, some companies are working on equipment that will be able to take vital signs and test for the use of alcohol and drugs. In addition, some of the equipment will determine that an offender has left the area where he or she is expected to remain, and this technology will instantly advise the offender that such movement has been detected by a visual display or a voice message. Some even have suggested that the equipment transmit a small chemical or electric shock to "get the offender's attention." So far, this is not technologically feasible; but science and technology are on the move. When such devices are readily available, users will have to deal with numerous issues of ethics and civil liberties as well as practical ramifications of the application.

Whatever the next generation of equipment turns out to be, there probably will be some repetition of the prior pattern. At the beginning, the equipment will have technological glitches. Over time, it will be refined and become more reliable. At the same time, articles will appear in the popular press and professional journals questioning the legality and morality of the use of the technology on offenders. One way or another, the equipment will come and the issues will be resolved, but we do not know how or when this will happen.

Electronic Monitoring Equipment Available

There are many kinds of equipment available for the monitoring of offenders. Here is a sampler, in no particular order:

1. BEEPERS—The offender is required to wear a standard, commercially available beeper through which the supervising officer periodically signals the offender to call the officer who is at a location with "Caller ID" on the telephone. This approach has the advantage that, if the officer knows the numbers at the place of employment and pay phones near where the offender lives, the offender can maintain program contact without having to have a telephone. If "Caller ID" is not available, then the offender can tell the officer the number from which he or she is calling, the officer can check to assure that this phone, probably a pay phone, is in an appropriate location and call the offender back to verify that he or she is at the number provided. In some instances of severe economic limitation, programs have established an 800 number so offenders are not charged for their calls to the program.

2. PROGRAMMED CONTACT DEVICES—A computer calls the offender on the telephone periodically to ensure that he or she is at the monitored location and verifies that the person responding is the one being monitored. Verification may be accomplished in a variety of ways, including but not limited to a device the offender wears and voice verification. A printout is produced which shows when the calls were made, whether the call was answered, and if verification occurred.

The methods described are relatively inexpensive to operate, but both have the disadvantage that they only verify the offender is home at the time the call is placed; there is no way to tell if he or she left one minute after receiving the call, gambling that it will be awhile before another call is made.

3. CONTINUOUSLY SIGNALING DEVICES—This type of equipment has three components: a transmitter worn by the offender which emits an encoded signal. The signal has a range of 100 to 200 feet and is received by a receiver-dialer installed at the monitored location to notify the central computer when the monitored person comes within or goes out of range of the unit. The central computer contains the offender's schedule and, when notified of a change in the person's status, compares the time with his or her schedule to determine if the break in contact is authorized. If not authorized, the computer sends an alert.

With this equipment, it is possible to determine whether or not the offender is home at any given time. However, the monitoring agency has no idea where the person is when not home or what he or she is doing when at home.

4. HYBRID EQUIPMENT—This is a combination of two of the types of equipment described. Hybrid equipment functions as a continuously signaling device until it notes the offender has left the monitored range at an unauthorized time. Then, it functions similarly to a programmed contact device by telephonically contacting the offender and verifying that the person responding to the call is the monitored offender. If verification does not occur, notification of the violation is made.

5. EQUIPMENT ENHANCEMENTS—In addition to the hybrid equipment, the continuously signaling equipment may be enhanced in several ways. One type offers an attachment which requires an offender to blow into a breathalyzer to give an indication of breath alcohol content from a long distance. Noninvasive methods of testing for the presence of illegal drugs have not yet been developed, but they are on the drawing board.

Another enhancement provides an apparatus by which the officer can receive the signal being sent out by the transmitter. This allows the officer to drive to the offender's home or place of employment and "tune into" the offender signal frequency so as to ascertain that the subject is there without leaving his car or physically intervening in the offender's activity.

Still another enhancement is the ability to program two receivers to one transmitter, thereby creating a system designed to monitor an offender at his or her home and detect the same offender if he or she approaches a second location. This gives an agency the ability to enforce restraining orders and deter an offender from confronting a victim. Some systems even provide a portable remote receiver designed to be carried by a victim in public places or taken to the person's workplace. If the offender's transmitter violates that receiver's perimeter, it activates an audible warning tone as long as the offender is in range.

Finally, some systems have officer safety pendants, designed to be used by supervisory personnel in the field. If confronted by a life-threatening situation, the officer activates the pendant which sends a signal to the receiver-dialer in the offender's home. This, in turn, alerts monitoring personnel of an "officer needs help" situation at that location.

As a generalization, programmed contact devices are less expensive than continuously signaling devices which are, in turn, less expensive than the hybrid equipment. Enhancements generally represent additional costs.

6. TRACKING ELECTRONIC MONITORING EQUIPMENT (TEM)—Tracking electronic monitoring is different from the continuously signaling equipment previously described in that it tracks the offender's location as he or she moves around the community. At this time, tracking electronic monitoring for use in cities is just becoming commercially available, so we cannot describe its configuration. However, it will probably include a transmitter which will periodically send a signal to devices located throughout a specified geographical area within which the offender is required to remain or to global positioning satellites. This will allow the offender's specific location within the area to be determined. As the offender moves, the path is plotted and may be compared with an approved route or location. There are a number of possible signal recipients including the cellular telephone system, receivers positioned specifically for this equipment, and the Global Positioning Satellite network.

Notes:

[1]Schwitzgebel (now Gable), R. K. et al. 1964. "A Program of Research in Behavior Electronics." *Behavioral Science.* 9: 233-238.

[2]Friel, Charles M., Joseph B. Vaughn, and Rolando del Carmen. *Electronic Monitoring and Correctional Policy: The Technology and Its Application.* NIJ Research Report, June 1987.

[3]Sherman, Lawrence W. "What's New in Prison Jewelry." *Wall Street Journal.* Friday, January 16, 1987, page 22.

[4]Ms. Connelly formerly worked for the Bureau of Prisons and is President and Chief Operating Officer of Linda Connelly and Associates, a criminal justice and social service agency.

[5]The Community Justice Coalition of Connecticut, Inc. (developed by) Irene Favreau, Executive Director. 1992. "Community Corrections Standards for Nonresidential Programs."

[6]*American Correctional Association Standards for Electronic Monitoring Programs.* Lanham, Maryland 1995.

[7]Advanced Business Sciences, Inc. 3335 North 107th Street, Omaha, Nebraska 68134, 402-498-2734.

[8]Pro Tech Monitoring, Inc., 1211 N. Westshore Blvd., Suite 416, Tampa, Florida 33607-4605, 813-286-1038.

[9]Murphy, John H. Undated. "Advanced Electronic Monitoring for Tracking Persons on Probation or Parole." Northrop Grumman Corporation, Pittsburgh, Pennsylvania.

[10]*Ibid*, page 33.

16

Electronic Monitoring in the Washington State Department of Corrections

David Savage

Director
State of Washington Department of Corrections
Division of Community Corrections
Olympia, Washington

The criminal justice system in the state of Washington has used electronic monitoring for a number of years. It has been used by many jurisdictions, primarily as an alternative to jail confinement. Although overall use in relation to the total jail population is not as high as in many other states, electronic monitoring has had a valued impact on jail space and as a sentence option.

The Washington State Department of Corrections, Division of Community Corrections, has a more recent and brief history with electronic monitoring. Our original interest was stirred by a desire to increase monitoring of more serious offenders supervised in the community with curfew conditions and as a sanction alternative to returning offenders to prison. The department contracts with the Washington Association of Sheriffs and Police Chiefs for electronic monitoring services. The primary benefit of this relationship has been the ability to provide electronic monitoring statewide, through local law enforcement, at reduced cost because of volume. This partnership also permits the department to keep up with the quickly changing technology.

Although the use of electronic monitoring by the department generally has been successful, we have not met the anticipated volume, and the scope of its use has changed. Electronic monitoring is currently used for the less serious offenders as an alternative to confinement when facing minor violations. Also, we implemented the use of electronic monitoring without the addition of specific funding to our budget in the belief that most of the cost could be recovered from the offenders paying for the service. This has proven an incorrect assumption attributable to the types of offenders and the circumstances under which they were placed on electronic monitoring. Not obtaining the levels of usage that were initially anticipated is partially due to the increased workload on individual community corrections officers and the lack of widespread acceptance of the use of electronic monitoring with the target offender population.

Electronic monitoring has the potential to free up community corrections officers from monitoring activities, information gathering, and administrative activities within their case management responsibility. As these words are being written, we are in the process of evaluating a Request for Proposal (RFP) to seek a private/public partnership with a potential vendor to develop a three-part "electronic monitoring model" made up of new hardware and software applications that will be the responsibility of the vendor to develop. We hope that the department will enter into a partnership with a private vendor that will lead to the development of three independent, but essentially linked, components.

The first component is a hardware and software application that will allow the gathering of information directly from offenders, freeing up the time community corrections officers spend gathering routine information. The model may resemble the KIOSK concept that has gained popularity in providing public interface with government functions across the nation. The second component is a Community Activity Monitoring System (CAMS) system, which has more flexibility than the traditional electronic monitoring system in monitoring offender activities in the community. Ideally, this system will allow community corrections officers to monitor the presence of offenders at home, work, treatment, or in meeting other conditions of their sentence. The third component is a community corrections officer work station. This component will provide the linkage of technology so that the KIOSK model, the CAMS model, and our existing Offender Based Tracking System (OBTS) and database can be linked together. This will allow systems to share information with each other and provide the community corrections officer with one point of input and retrieval for a variety of information, previously obtainable only through making numerous data inquiries.

If we and our private partner are successful, we envision technology freeing up community corrections officers' time to spend providing meaningful intervention and quality programs directly to offenders. Pursuing this future through a public/private partnership, although not new to state government, is new in the Washington State Department of Corrections. The anticipated advantages of pursuing this objective through a public/private partnership is the potential to have considerable influence in meeting our specific needs by being a partner, as well as the potential of a lesser cost in comparison to purchasing similar products or services on the open market.

Although our immediate experience with electronic monitoring from a traditional perspective has not been exactly what we had hoped, we are excited about our future in relation to electronic monitoring. We look forward to being a partner in its development.

17

Is Electronic Home Monitoring a Viable Option?

Ray Wahl

Director of Field Operations
Utah Department of Corrections
Murray, Utah

Using electronic monitoring devices to supervise offenders emerged as a topic for discussion throughout the criminal justice field in 1978. Today, more than 10,000 offenders wear monitoring devices, and even the most traditional agencies employ these tools to combat crowded jails, enhance supervision techniques, monitor house arrest, and punish. Provided agencies follow certain guidelines, their legal concerns about the use of electronic monitoring will remain few. However, is this equipment used effectively? When does monitoring become a costly intrusion to offenders and a superfluous addition to correctional agencies?

Many officials are not clear about why they are using electronic monitoring. Recent evaluations reveal substantial differences in the ways institutions throughout the country employ this technique; some regard electronic monitoring as a sentence, while others see it as a supplement to one. Every agency fits its electronic monitoring program into its own structure; therefore, criteria, policy, and operations surrounding its use differ. Although many report that it is an effective alternative to prison crowding and an excellent addition to supervision practices, some administrations are widening the net of social control and placing people under supervision who ordinarily would not warrant or deserve this security.

Clearly, there are instances when using monitoring devices is inappropriate. For example, is it necessary to electronically chaperon an offender convicted of driving while intoxicated? To do so might result in violation of the offender's privacy and in needless cost for the offender as well as for the agency. It is all too tempting to employ the equipment simply because the means are available to do so. A national examination of correctional facilities is needed to establish whether electronic monitoring is used appropriately or if, in fact, it has become a tool for some agencies to exert undue social control.

Issues to Consider

Properly and efficiently employed, electronic monitoring equipment becomes a useful tool to correctional officials who address key issues before implementing the system. Each agency should first determine if and when this type of guarding is necessary to protect society and/or rehabilitate an offender. Often, it is assumed that a person under electronic monitoring would otherwise have gone to jail. Is this necessarily the case, though? If not, it becomes an unnecessary expense.

Once the purpose for employing it is established, officials then can decide what equipment is necessary to accomplish this goal and if a service provider is needed to monitor it. Perhaps in-house staff preclude the need to hire a provider. Likewise, officials need to consider if it is more efficient to purchase the equipment or to lease it and, more importantly, who will pay to use it. Legal problems may result from the practice of excluding applicants from the program because they cannot pay the service fees or because they do not have access to a phone. Many offenders cannot afford electronic monitoring and should be given the opportunity to use it regardless of their financial status. Providing the service on a sliding-scale basis ensures that this alternative does not become an option only for the rich offender. Furthermore, many systems lie dormant because local courts and law enforcers do not support electronic monitoring programs. Getting the cooperation from those in the legal system is paramount. Electronic monitoring becomes a burden to agencies whose local judge does not support it and refuses to order offenders to use it.

After deciding when to use electronic monitoring, who will pay to use it, and where to purchase the equipment, program supervisors should write a contract holding a vendor responsible for the equipment yet allowing officials to cancel the contract, if necessary. It is also important to include a severability clause in contracts that addresses the issues of equipment reliability, repair, and mailing of the apparatus. Purchasers can avoid many problems by conferring with other users of electronic monitoring systems. Correctional officials who decide to use this type of system in their programs can follow their research with a written method of how to evaluate systems. It is essential, therefore, that all agencies implementing electronic monitoring systems study each issue before becoming involved in it rather that asking questions of vendors or, worse yet, asking questions after investing time and money into the program.

Most investigators considering electronic monitoring are concerned with cost effectiveness and typically compare the cost of incarceration to the cost of the electronic monitoring equipment. Rarely estimated, though, is the cost of staff time and training, administrative overview, and supervision time. The system is often only an economical option if it is used to monitor an individual who otherwise would have been sentenced to jail. Electronic monitoring can be attractive because it may prove to be less expensive than other programs, depending on its purpose, participants, and operation. However, it will survive as a correctional alternative not because it is cheaper but because it is a useful substitute for and enhancement of supervision.

References

EMT Group. 1987. Electronic Monitoring Programs: An Overview. *Offender Monitoring.* Vol. 1, No. 1.

Enos, Richard, Clifford Black, James F. Quinn, and John Holman. 1992. *Alternative Sentencing: Electronically Monitored Correctional Supervision.* Bristol, Indiana: Wyndam Hall Press.

Petersilia, Joan. 1986. Exploring the Options of House Arrest. *Federal Probation* I. June.

Rush, George F. 1987. Electronic Monitoring: An Alternative to Incarceration. Paper presented at the 42nd International Conference of the Correctional Education Association, July.

Electronic Monitoring's Place in Community Corrections: A Canadian Perspective

Terrance F. Lang

Director of Community Operations
Department of Justice
Saskatchewan, Canada

If you listen to the media, prison still seems to be the preferred sentence for every criminal offense except for murder, when many lobby for something more harsh than prison. Anything less than incarceration is viewed as being soft on crime, a charge that has fueled many political campaigns.

Is there a role for community-based sanctions within this atmosphere? The answer is "yes." Community-based sanctions need to be seen as tough and credible within the community and the criminal justice system. They also have a role to play in shifting the public's mind-set about appropriate responses to crime.

Justice Edward Culliton of the Saskatchewan Court of Appeal said there should be a constant changing of approach to sentencing—concepts of retribution and deterrence being gradually replaced by rational social science concepts. "Such a changing attitude requires, from time to time, a review and reappraisal of both the elements underlying an appropriate sentence and the emphasis to be placed thereon."

Range of Sanctions

This paper focuses primarily on intensive probation combined with electronic monitoring initiatives.

Most states in the United States and most provinces in Canada have developed an array of community-based sentencing options ranging from fines, probation, supervision, restitution, community service, and attendance centers to intensive supervision and electronic monitoring programs. These options can be described as a "continuum of control" ranging from minimal punishment or intrusion into an offender's life (such as a fine) to very extensive intrusion, control, and supervision that is just shy of the amount of control provided in an institutional setting.

Two Saskatchewan judges' statements support this argument. In R. V. Foster, a 1991 drug trafficking case, justice C. R. Wimmer of the Court of Queen's Bench said:

> In my judgment, imprisonment does not necessarily require confinement to an institution constructed for that purpose. Jails are not made only of walls and fences. It strikes me that total confinement to one's residence represents a serious loss of liberty and is in itself a term of imprisonment.

In April 1993, Justice W. J. Vancise of the Saskatchewan Court of Appeal wrote in a paper presented to an Electronic Monitoring Conference in Vancouver:

> Until the development of the technology to permit the electronic monitoring of an offender confined to a residence, there had not been an effective sanction as an alternative to imprisonment in the array of sentencing options acceptable to the public. In this context, "effective" means sufficiently intrusive, demeaning and perceived by the public to be punitive. Electronically monitored house arrest is a sanction with sufficient punitive elements (restrictive of liberty and autonomy) to be an acceptable alternative for imprisonment. It is not a panacea, and must not be regarded as a sanction which will empty jails, but it can be an effective alternative to the sentencing options available to the courts. It may also be the catalyst which will force the courts to examine and re-examine the effectiveness of the traditional custodial sentence as punishment for nonviolent crimes.

This last statement directs the criminal justice system to rethink what it considers "appropriate" sanctions. If we can design and deliver more effective, safe, and responsible alternatives to jail, we will shift perceptions and thus practices of sentencing.

Saskatchewan's Program

The Saskatchewan Intensive Probation Supervision/Electronic Monitoring Program (IPSEM) is beginning to influence sentencing practices in the province. Started in January 1990, IPSEM is a "front-end" program—the assessment and decision to place someone in this program is made by the courts as part of the sentence. It is not an administrative release mechanism from a custodial sentence.

It is important to point out that this is not simply an electronic monitoring program. It is an intensive probation program that provides professional supervision and counseling to promote responsible behavior. Electronic monitoring is seen as part of the intensive supervision program for offenders requiring an additional level of control or supervision.

Critical to this sanction is the ability to properly assess the offender and his or her environment through a presentence report, and to develop a specific, detailed case plan for the offender while on the intensive probation program. Offenders must be directed to examine and work on the problems and needs that contributed to illegal behavior. For example, they must deal with their alcohol or drug abuse or take sex-offender treatment if these problems are related to the offense. Simply placing someone on electronic monitoring twenty-four hours a day and doing nothing to address his or her needs will have minimal long-term effect. The time must be used to deal with criminogenic behavior.

Intensive probation with electronic monitoring is a sanction at the upper level of the continuum of control. It is a sanction that combines some elements of imprisonment—restriction of liberty by confining offenders to their residence—with a high level of community-based programming service and supervision.

Saskatchewan evaluated the first year of program operation (1990-91). This was not an in-depth study looking at recidivism and effectiveness, but primarily an administrative review measured against the program' goals. The study, which looked at 201 offenders who were referred to or considered for the Intensive Probation Supervision/Electronic Monitoring Program, provides some data on the offense and offender profiles. The data showed the following crime-related characteristics:

- 29 percent were offenses against persons (assaults, sex offenses, robbery weapons)
- 10 percent were drug-related offenses (possession for the purpose of trafficking
- 35 percent were property offenses
- 26 percent were other offenses (such as failure to appear and drunk driving)

Of the 201 referrals, 46 percent had previously been incarcerated and 77 percent had previous criminal records. A total of 94 of the 201 offenders were actually placed on intensive probation/electronic monitoring following assessment through the presentence report and sentencing by the courts.

When the program was designed, individuals with eight "high-profile" offenses were not expected to be considered for the program, These were homicide, prison breach, sexual assault with a weapon, aggravated sexual assault, abduction, assault with a weapon, aggravated assault, and breaking and entering with intent to commit one of these offenses. As it turned out, however, 12 percent of the offenses considered were these high-profile offenses. This is not to say electronic monitoring is appropriate for all offenders convicted of these serious offenses. Rather, this sanction my be appropriate for selected offenders whose circumstances warrant a noncustodial sentence.

Two of the largest groups identified when the program began were women and aboriginal offenders. During the first year of operation, women constituted about 31 percent of referrals and aboriginal offenders accounted for 39 percent of referrals.

Overall, intensive probation supervision without electronic monitoring was ordered in 23 percent of the cases. Intensive probation with electronic monitoring was ordered in 77 percent of the cases.

Six of the 94 offenders (6.4 percent) released in the program committed new crimes. This is very low considering the type of offenders and nature of offenses. As expected, a significant number of offenders (40 percent) violated some of the conditions—normally the curfew conditions and the alcohol or substance abuse conditions—and received sanctions ranging from a warning to a new charge.

The researcher, Shaukat Nasim of the Saskatchewan Department of Justice, concluded:

> The intensive probation supervision/electronic monitoring program was a success with respect to the low recidivism rate of only 6.4 percent. Therefore, the offenders released on the program did not pose an unnecessary risk to society. Although the violation (of condition) rate was 40 percent, the community at large was not unduly threatened in any known way by the violations of curfew and/or the consumption of alcohol. In these cases, the probation officer took prompt action and charged a majority of the violators with new offenses.

It is important to emphasize the need for prompt and appropriate action in response to violations. Probation officers are on call twenty-four hours a day and receive alarm notices immediately through pagers. Saskatchewan has had excellent cooperation and support from area police departments and the Royal Canadian Mounted Police. They respond very quickly to violations and, in many cases, have the offender in court the next day.

One early criticism of electronic monitoring was that it was a "middle class" option because offenders needed a stable residence with a telephone. Saskatchewan has overcome this in a number of ways. While it is true the offender requires some form of stable residence, in some cases this has been accommodated through the use of hostels, such as those run by the Salvation Army. If the offender is indigent and cannot afford a telephone or cannot obtain a telephone due to unpaid telephone bills, the Department of Justice will install and pay for a telephone in cooperation with the telephone company. Doing this is less expensive than incarcerating an offender who cannot afford to pay. In addition, Saskatchewan has contracted with a number of service providers who provide supervision and support to offenders in the outlying communities. Often, this supervision displaces the need for electronic monitoring.

The Saskatchewan Intensive Probation Supervision/Electronic Monitoring Program provides a credible sentencing option that addresses the need for punishment and deterrence while providing an excellent opportunity for offender rehabilitation. Community sanctions can be tailored to meet the needs of the offender, control the risk of reoffending, and provide an acceptable level of protection to the community.

Justice Vancise, in addressing the question of whether the courts can impose alternatives to incarceration when a custodial sentence would normally be imposed and still maintain confidence in the administration of justice, said:

> I believe that not only are the courts able to, but that noncustodial alternative sentences can be rationalized and justified and indeed, that confidence in the administration of justice will not only be maintained, but enhanced. The intermediate sentence of electronically monitoring the offender's confinement to a residence is perfectly suited to replace incarceration as an appropriate sentence for nonviolent crimes, in combination where necessarywith intensive supervision and other penalties such as community service orders where appropriate. The courts must determine what is a fit sentence having regard to all sentencing options and sanctions available.

▼19

Electronic Monitoring:
From Innovation, to
Routine, to Anticipation

Jim Putnam

Administrator
Michigan Department of Corrections
Office of Residential and Electronic Programs
Lansing, Michigan

S ome devices once viewed as innovations quickly are taken for granted. Few remember that televisions, fax machines, and car phones were once considered technological novelties. Now, most of us wonder how people survived without them. Electronic monitoring systems are another of the technological wonders that have become routine.

The Birth of a Program

In 1986, the Michigan Department of Corrections ventured into a technological wasteland, joining with B. I., Inc. to put in place an effective active electronic monitoring system. By April, a demonstration project in Washtenaw County was unveiled.

The project was restricted to felony probationers. The goal was to show that the equipment worked, and that offenders could be monitored effectively. During the demonstration, the equipment was modified many times. The department's Bureau of Field Services' staff and company engineers quickly became experts in radio technology. We learned, for example, that houses sometimes have "dead zones"—small pockets where the transmitter cannot send its signal—and that an FM radio station can interfere with electronic monitoring. However, the engineers eventually worked out all the bugs and, a year and a half after the demonstration began, we put it into use statewide. The program was offered for three types of offenders: felony probationers, inmates participating in the Community Residential Program (CRP), and parolees. Since that initial offering, the program has expanded and is now offered to any governmental unit.

A Slow but Steady Acceptance

Initially, most people—including judges and correctional officials—were skeptical of the electronic monitoring systems. Electronic monitoring services were offered as a sentencing option to all circuit courts in Michigan. Our intention was to divert from prison appropriate offenders, those who did not present a threat to society. The initial response was underwhelming, to say the least. It soon became clear that judges were not willing to rely on an untested technology for monitoring a felon who otherwise would be in prison. We made gaining their acceptance our goal.

The department started by encouraging probation agents to recommend electronic monitoring as an enhancement to court-ordered supervision, giving judges enough exposure to the system to become comfortable with it. We felt that, like the fax machine, comfort would become reliance. Also, we avoided the risk of having an offender who would have been incarcerated commit a new crime.

In Genesee County, we tried using transmitters with an intensive supervision unit which targeted newly convicted felony offenders with histories of substance abuse. Each agent in the program had a reduced number of probationers to supervise. Urine testing for substance abuse was done on a frequent, but irregular, basis. The program gained the support of local judges, and there is now a waiting list of offenders for the program. Said Genesee County Judge Earl E. Borradaile, "When staff can monitor offenders closely, it is a great program."

The probation electronic monitoring program began to be used statewide. Now, ankle bracelets are accepted as an effective and invaluable correctional tool. Judges responding to a survey reported that they had used electronic monitoring as a sentence condition, and they considered it a potential alternative to jail or prison.

In Michigan, there are more than 3,000 offenders on the state's electronic monitoring systems. Compliance has exceeded expectations: less than 5 percent of all offenders have escaped, and less than 2 percent of offenders have been arrested again. Currently, there are more than 1,600 felony probationers wearing electronic monitors in Michigan. We expect there to be more next year. Many of these offenders would otherwise be living in the state's crowded facilities.

The Community Residential Program

Michigan has had a Community Residential Program for inmates for more than twenty years. Participation is based on the nature of their crime, eligibility for parole, criminal history, institutional conduct, and psychological history. Excluded from the program are sex offenders and people with histories of sex offenses, major drug dealers, members of organized crime, and offenders with a pattern of assault or those classified as potentially very assaultive.

Most of the offenders in the Community Residential Program are placed in state-run facilities near their homes, and these facilities have twenty-four-hour staff on duty. Offenders are expected to get a job, reestablish home and family ties, and build a sound basis for parole release. Once they have a job and a potential residence, they are eligible for parole. Following the 1986 Washtenaw demonstration project, Community Residential Program inmates living at home received electronic monitors. Here, electronic monitoring was not used to divert people from returning to prison; rather, it was used to enhance the existing program's supervision. Staff visits to homes were reduced because it was no longer necessary to use agents to confirm what electronic monitoring systems automatically reported. State law now requires that any prisoner in a community program must either be in a residential facility or on electronic monitoring. Today, there are more than 900 community-status prisoners on electronic monitoring.

Community Residential Program offenders have forced us to improve some electronic monitoring equipment. The devices have an alarm that is designed to alert monitors if offenders attempt to tamper with them. However, some offenders figured out that by using heating pads, hot water bottles, or hair dryers they could stretch the bracelets without triggering the alarm. They could then remove their bracelets and leave them at home while they went out. One inmate used glue to rebuild his anklet. In the end, with equipment changes, the system prevailed. Offenders realized that, even though a correctional officer was not with them, curfew and tamper violations would be discovered and penalties would be imposed.

Parole has made limited use of the electronic monitoring system. Currently, there are fewer than 200 parolees on the system. It is used for parolees who have completed the department's Boot Camp program and is routinely considered for technical rule violators as an alternative to returning them to prison. William J. Hudson, former chairman of the Michigan Parole Board, said, "While electronic monitoring is obviously not for every case, it should be a consideration in every case. It is part of good case management. . . ."

Other Uses for Electronic Monitoring Systems

In Michigan, electronic monitoring sometimes is used for low-risk felony offenders, juveniles in the care of the Department of Social Services, and misdemeanor offenders. With crowded jails in several counties, electronic monitoring provides an alternative to jail incarceration for low-risk offenders who are sentenced to jail, making more jail beds available for higher-risk misdemeanor and felony offenders. The department has contracted with eighteen agencies in thirteen counties for electronic monitoring services, with more contracts pending. Contracts with counties for adult offenders have resulted in judges using electronic monitoring as a sentencing option for selected bond cases, when reducing a sentence for good behavior, in conjunction with day release programs, and as an alternative to monitoring some hospitalized inmates.

The accelerating use of electronic monitoring clearly demonstrates that it is no longer an innovation on trial. It is effective and deserves to be solidly entrenched as a case management tool. Like the word processor on which this article was written, yesterday's innovation is part of today's routine.

Anticipation

In 1986, when we began looking at electronic monitoring systems, the department's budget was approximately $375 million. Since then, the public has decided to get tough on criminals. The "get tough" initiatives such as "Three Strikes and You're Out," or "Truth in Sentencing" have resulted in a prison population explosion. Thanks to diversion resources like the electronic monitoring systems, among others, commitment rates in Michigan are actually down. However, because of longer sentences, prison population is increasing. The department's budget is now more than $1.2 billion. Corrections will compete seriously with educational and social programs for a major share of the state's budget dollars, forcing officials to make difficult decisions about the sharing of limited resources.

This author anticipates that during the next three to four years, the next generation of electronic monitoring equipment will substantially alter corrections. Currently in development are systems which use "real time tracking"—the ability to track an offender regardless of location twenty-four hours a day. This will allow us to create an electronic prison within the community. Prisoners can be confined to their homes and to specified electronic corridors for travel to employment. Violations would be responded to immediately, just as we do with the current limited system. This would allow nearly all nonassaultive offenders to be diverted from prison.

The potential cost savings are enormous. Currently, Michigan spends less than $7 per day to supervise an offender on electronic monitoring. Even if the new system costs three times that amount, it is far cheaper than prison and eliminates the issue of massive prison construction as a bonus. There are several companies working on such a system. The first one in the pool wins a big prize!

Electronically Monitored Home Confinement

Perry Johnson

Corrections Consultant
Holt, Michigan

In 1979, the Michigan legislature enacted an Emergency Powers Act (EPA) aimed at controlling the state's prison population until additional prison space could be built. This Act empowered the governor to reduce inmates' sentences by ninety days whenever prisons became crowded. It worked for a time, but growing public opposition soon made the Emergency Powers Act politically untenable. In the fall of 1984, the governor announced that he would not use the Act again but, instead, would support a prison building program. The Act was subsequently repealed. Michigan's prison population nearly tripled by the mid-1990s while more than a billion dollars was spent on prison construction. This prison housing crisis provided the impetus for electronic monitoring.

Shortly after the demise of the Emergency Powers Act, community corrections—which might have offered relief for the bulging prisons—also fell on hard times. Sensational media accounts of crimes committed by parolees and halfway house inmates undermined the credibility of these programs. Consequently, the parole board was reconstituted from civil service status to political appointees. Halfway house beds became even more difficult to acquire. Political pressures, arising from the perception by the media and the public that the programs were unsafe, resulted in the legislative leadership serving notice that a house arrest program for 800 inmates (called "extended furlough") must be eliminated. This would have added these inmates to already crowded prisons. The leadership, however, agreed to consider electronically monitored home confinement as an alternative for extended furlough. It was their opinion that individual legislators would be able to equate constant electronic surveillance with on-site halfway house supervision when responding to concerned constituents.

A Social Experiment

These two political decisions, the elimination of the Emergency Powers Act and extended furlough, became the driving forces behind the speed and extent to which electronic monitoring was developed in Michigan. They provided a social experiment that otherwise would not have existed.

The genesis for the concept of electronically monitored home confinement in Michigan came from "intensive supervision" probation programs already piloted in Florida, Georgia, and New Jersey. Michigan hoped to provide better offender monitoring at lower cost through the use of technology. Two offender populations were targeted for electronically monitored home confinement:

- inmates qualified for the former extended furlough status (called "prisoner home confinement" for purposes of this article)
- convicted felons who would receive a prison or jail sentence if electronic moitoring were not available (called "probation home confinement")

In both instances, the alternative to the home confinement program would be jail, prison, or a halfway house. Both were intended to relieve prison crowding, not to enhance existing community supervision.

The probation home confinement program was offered to the courts with two stipulations:

- The offender must be employed or attending an approved training or education program within sixty days unless prohibited by a medical condition or the probation order.
- The field agent shall recommend to the court that reimbursement be ordered that will not exceed 50 percent of the offender's net pay, and that any remaining cost balance be provided by community service work.

The department promised the courts that continuously signaling electronic monitoring combined with intensive field supervision would be provided. More than 1,500 offenders were in the program by December, 1995.

The Prisoner Home Confinement Program

Electronic monitoring alone is not a program. It is merely one element of a program. The five important elements of the prisoner home confinement program include the following:

1. a classification system using actuarial risk prediction to screen out the most violent inmates

2. a continuously signaling electronically monitored curfew

3. biweekly substance abuse testing

4. an emphasis on employment

5. caseloads under thirty per agent

Classification is absolutely critical to the success of any community corrections program. A classification system should be a blend of common sense, political reality, and statistical risk prediction. Common sense is necessary because it is important that staff, the criminal justice community, and the public understand and support the system. Political encouragement, or at least the absence of political opposition, is essential for the program to exist, and the program must be reasonably safe if it is to survive. Statistical risk prediction is the best means available to assess offender dangerousness.

Some challenge the appropriateness of using statistical risk prediction, claiming it is unreliable and unjust, but Michigan has found it possible to predict violence potential. Objective factors predicting assaultive crimes were first used in parole and prison classification in June, 1976, and the research has been validated and replicated many times since. Classification is a necessary part of modern corrections and, because actuarial methods are the most objective means available, justice is enhanced, not diminished, by their use.

Classification does not mean that only the very best cases are skimmed off—it means that only a few will qualify. Many offenders with multiple felony convictions or who were serving time for robbery, burglary, and other serious crimes have performed very well in the prisoner home confinement program. Still, there are criminals so dangerous, persistent, or unmanageable that they could never be controlled in a community corrections program. That is why those with poor institutional behavior, demonstrated escape proneness, or who have a high risk of violent recidivism must be screened out.

The second program element, continuously signaling electronic monitoring, is used to ensure inmate compliance with curfew requirements. Each offender in the program is required to wear a small FM transmitter that is mated to a receiver/telephone dialer placed in the residence. A host computer at a remote location monitors the offender's presence or absence. Any attempt to remove the transmitter or tamper with the receiver results in a tamper alarm at the host computer. The host computer is programmed to allow for absences for work or other approved activities. Employed inmates are required to pay the rental cost for the electronic monitoring devices, but not in excess of one-half of their earnings.

The third element is substance abuse testing. All inmates in the program are required to submit to biweekly testing for drug abuse, and violators are removed from the program. This may seem arbitrary; however, mandatory testing with certain consequences does deter illegal drug use.

The fourth element is an emphasis on employment for the able bodied. Where possible, the employed are given priority consideration for placement in the program. Unemployed inmates are allowed no more than sixty days to find employment and are required to seek work between 8:00 A.M. and 1:00 P.M. on weekdays. Another important factor in job finding is to make it the inmate's responsibility and not a staff obligation. Too often in the past, offenders have reversed that responsibility and then found excuses to avoid every job that was found by staff. So far, no one has been returned for failing to get a job.

Finally, caseloads for the program should not exceed thirty per agent. This allows for at least weekly personal contact, biweekly drug testing, and confirmation of inmate employment, along with the agents' other supervision duties.

Program Cost and Performance

The net annual cost per offender for fiscal year 1995 was $1,263—$500 for equipment and operations plus $2,011 for field staff minus offender contributions of $1,248. The annual cost of minimum security confinement, the cheapest institutional alternative to home confinement, is more than ten times as much ($15,000). This difference has major budget implications. Consider, for example, that by December, 1995, just one-hundred months after the Michigan program inception, 900 prison inmates and 1,750 felony probationers or parolees were under electronic monitoring. If we assume that, absent electronically monitored home confinement, at least two-thirds of these offenders would have been housed in minimum-security prisons, jails, or halfway houses, then the Michigan taxpayer savings in 1995 exceeded 25 million dollars.

Some will say, however, that the added safety of keeping these offenders out of the community a few more months was worth the expense. During 1995, more than 10,000 offenders passed through Michigan's electronic monitoring program, with an average stay of just over three months, and the total new felony arrests for this group was 194. That is just 2 percent. It is likely that many of these 194 arrests would have occurred following more conventional release three months later, even if they were not on electronic monitoring. This is a bargain for the taxpayer.

Recommendations

Electronic monitoring is not for all offenders. It is most appropriate as an adjunct to the conventional halfway house for placement of offenders (either probationers or inmates) who have obtained employment and remain drug free. Those who are unwilling or unable to comply with program restrictions, people out of control because of serious psychological problems, and the very dangerous simply must be screened out of the program.

On the other hand, situational offenders and others with a law-abiding orientation do not require this level of supervision. Traditional probation with appropriate probation cases works just fine. However, for a significant segment of the offender group, a program that insists that they work, remain drug free, and stay home during high-risk leisure hours should reduce public risk to an acceptable level while imposing needed structure and control.

There is a common law adage that holds, "A man's home is his castle." That is now changing to, "A man's home is his prison." Could this be a harbinger of the impact of crime on contemporary society? Let us hope not. So long as criminals are the ones imprisoned in their homes to prevent crime, rather than citizens who are imprisoned in their homes from fear of crime, society will be well served.